The Logo Brainstorm Book

The Logo
Brainstorm
A Comprehensive
Guide for Exploring
Design Directions
Book

Jim Krause

HOW
BOOKS

Cincinnati, Ohio
www.howdesign.com

For more excellent books and resources for designers, visit www.howdesign.com.

16 15 14 13 12   5 4 3 2 1

ISBN-13: 978-1-4403-0431-6

Distributed in Canada by Fraser Direct
100 Armstrong Avenue
Georgetown, Ontario, Canada L7G 5S4
Tel: (905) 877-4411

Distributed in the U.K. and Europe by F&W Media International, LTD
Brunel House, Forde Close, Newton Abbot, TQ12 4PU, UK
Tel: (+44) 1626 323200, Fax: (+44) 1626 323319
Email: enquiries@fwmedia.com

Distributed in Australia by Capricorn Link
P.O. Box 704, Windsor, NSW 2756 Australia
Tel: (02) 4577-3555

Edited by Lauren Mosko Bailey and Amy Owen
Designed by Jim Krause
Art directed by Grace Ring
Production coordinated by Greg Nock

About the author:

Jim Krause has worked as a designer/illustrator/photographer in

the Pacific Northwest since the 1980s. He has produced award-

winning work for clients large and small and is the author and creator

of over a dozen books for creative professionals, including

Idea Index, Layout Index, Color Index, Color Index 2, Typography Index,

Design Basics Index, Photo Idea Index, Photo Idea Index: People,

Photo Idea Index: Places and *Photo Idea Index: Things.*

WWW.JIMKRAUSEDESIGN.COM

Table of contents

Introduction

I f you are anything like me, then one of the first things you want to know when you pick up a book about a well-covered topic (such as logo design) is this: What makes this book different from all the others? It's a fair question, and let me begin by answering it. *The Logo Brainstorm Book*—unlike the vast majority of books on the subject—is not filled with samples of logos. Granted, this may look like a book full of logo samples, but don't let appearances fool you: This is a book of suggestions, or, to put it as accurately as possible, this is a collection of idea-starters meant to help designers brainstorm their way to unique, attractive and effective logo solutions.

To understand how *The Logo Brainstorm Book* works, it helps to understand the degree to which—as well as the ways in which—designers are susceptible to the power of suggestion. What we're talking about here are the ways in which designers readily absorb ideas and inspiration from the things they encounter in everyday life: things like the swooping curve of sports car's fender, the expressive structure of a modern office building, the communicative conveyances of a sign's lettering or the muted hues of a woven scarf. Designers look at these things and, as long as they are paying attention at all, they can hardly help but be influenced by the visual, communicative and aesthetic suggestions of what they see—especially if those suggestions can somehow be applied to a creative project that is currently in the works.

Given this healthy propensity to draw ideas and inspiration from their surroundings, *The Logo Brainstorm Book* aspires to aid designers in the conceptualization and creation of logos by putting before their eyes page after page of logo-related aesthetic, stylistic and thematic suggestions. For example, take a quick look at pages 102–103. On this

1

Introduction

spread you will see a bunch of different renderings based on the human head, along with captions and text related to the images. The renderings on this spread could be used in all kinds of logo-developing ways. For starters, a designer might look at the pages and suddenly realize that a human-based icon might be just the thing needed for the logo she's working on. A designer could also use the spread's images to help brainstorm for different ways of stylizing a logo's icon—regardless of whether the icon is supposed to depict a human head or a head of cabbage. The spread's captions could be consulted for additional insights into the thinking behind the images or they could be read as stand-alone brainstorming prompts and melded with whatever ideas the designer already has brewing.

These are only a few ways that designers might use *The Logo Brainstorm Book.* The real point is that when designers open this book, engage with its content, blend what they see and read with their own ideas and preferences, and set about to develop concepts into presentation-ready material using whatever skills they possess and whatever tools they prefer, good things are bound to happen (and never more so than when the designers who use *The Logo Brainstorm Book* push hard enough to develop their ideas into finished designs that bear little or no resemblance to whatever images or words played a part in launching their creation).

The Logo Brainstorm Book is divided into seven chapters. The book opens with a chapter called Beginnings and this section covers three stages that can be used to get logo projects off to an efficient and well-targeted start: a stage where information is gathered, a stage where ideas are generated and a stage where visuals are developed and prepared for presentation. The next five chapters, Symbols, Monograms, Typographic Logos, Type + Symbol and Emblems, deal with different kinds of logos and logo elements that can be explored en route to coming up with finished designs. (If you are aiming to produce a particular style of logo, consider beginning your search for ideas in the chapter that best fits the description of what you're working on, and then be sure to move on to the book's other chapters: You never know when, for instance, a sample of a typographic treatment might spark an idea that leads to an effective symbol or monogram design. The book's final chapter, Color, provides information and ideas about selecting and applying colors to logo designs.

A quick word about tools before wrapping up this introduction. You will notice that this book often refers to three Adobe products: Illustrator, Photoshop and InDesign. Why include so many references to these particular products and so many tips related to their use? It's because these programs are, by far, the most commonly used logo-building tools on the planet, and to ignore the way that they can be used to create logos would be like trying to describe how to bake cupcakes without mentioning flour, sugar or ovens. If you use other kinds of software for your work, then feel free to adapt the Adobe-specific information to fit the capabilities of the programs you employ (and know that the ideas offered through the book's text and images have much to offer—regardless of what digital or hands-on tools you use to produce your work).

Thank you for picking up a copy of *The Logo Brainstorm Book.* I hope its content will help streamline your creative process while enhancing and expanding the range and quality of your work.

Jim Krause, WWW.JIMKRAUSEDESIGN.COM

1 Beginnings

CHAPTER CONTENTS

1   Beginnings

BUILDING A HOUSE is important business. Houses are meant to appeal to buyers through their aesthetics and functionality, houses should resist the forces of nature and houses ought to be constructed so that they will last a long time. A wise builder would never begin construction on a house without first looking into the tastes of its potential buyers, without coming up with a solid blueprint and without taking stock of all the materials and supplies needed for the project.

    Logo design, as it turns out, has a lot in common with home building: Logos should be aesthetically appealing and functionally capable, logos need to attract the attention of their

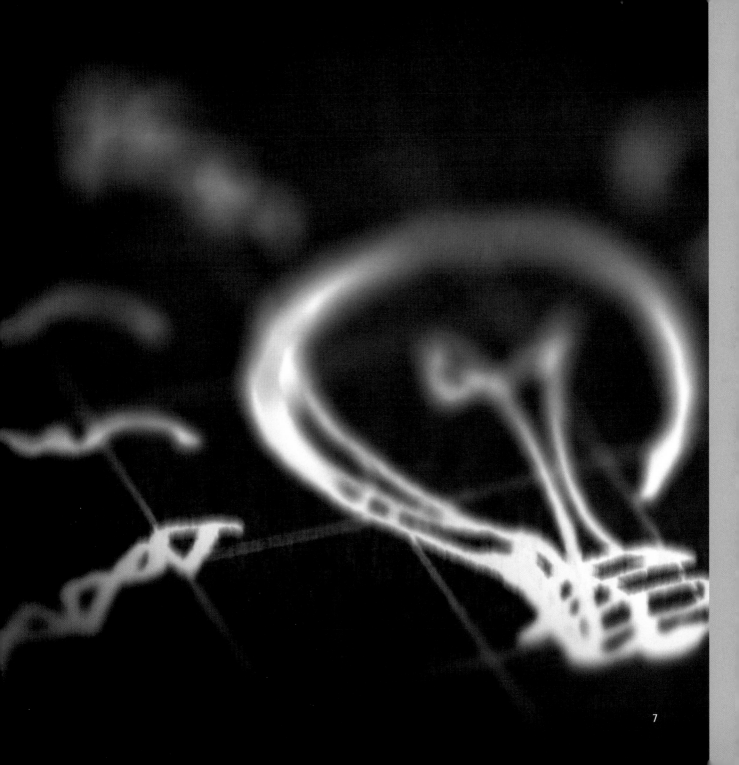

target audience and logos ought to be resilient against the winds of fad and fashion.

Do you want the logo you're about to build to appeal, function and last? Do you want the construction process to be as efficient, enjoyable and on-target as possible? Then you've got to prepare for the work ahead by gathering insight into the tastes of the people who will be paying for your design, the preferences of the audience who will be viewing it, the ways in which it will be used, the environments in which it will appear, the materials and tools that could be used to produce it and the means by which it could be constructed.

If this sounds like a demanding list of things to take into account when developing a logo, you're right. It is a sizable list, but it's also a reasonable and manageable accounting of what it will take to initiate your next logo-building project and to improve your chances of coming up with a successful design.

This chapter is dedicated to information-gathering, idea-expanding and design-developing processes that can be used to begin and guide your work when producing logo designs. Consider melding the creative practices described here with your own best ways of coming up with ideas and converting them into real-world visuals.

The creative practices described in this chapter are outlined from the point of view of freelance designers who meet directly with their clients. If your work situation involves go-betweens that interact with the client and pass information along to you (as in the case of a design agency's account executives or marketing people who act as intermediaries), then adapt what you read here to fit the reality of your workplace.

KNOW THY CLIENT

You know you've reached the end of a successful logo project when—after all is said, done and sold—you find yourself looking at a design that pleases the client, a design that is likely to excite and engage its target audience, a design that stands apart from anything a competitor is using and a design that makes you happy. Getting from the blank-page beginning of a project to this satisfying end is no easy task, but getting there can be made easier and much more of a sure thing when an effort is made—from the beginning of the job onward—to take into account the wishes of the client, the tastes of the target audience and the need to produce a design that stands out from the crowd.

Where to begin? By gaining an understanding of the client's tastes, preferences and expectations. Why start there? Because the reality of the situation is that it's the client who will be paying for the logo, and unless your design satisfies their aesthetic

Where to begin? By gaining an understanding of the client's tastes, preferences and expectations. Why start there? Because the reality of the situation is that it's the client who will be paying for the logo, and unless your design satisfies their aesthetic tastes and practical needs, then neither the client's target audience nor their competitors will ever get the chance to see your creation.

tastes and practical needs, then neither the client's target audience nor their competitors will ever get the chance to see your creation.

It's an excellent idea to begin any logo project by prompting revealing and idea-generating discussions with the client and listening to what they have to say:

- Find out as many details as you can about the products your client produces and the services they provide. Talk with the client about the tools of their trade and the ways they go about doing what they do. Ask for brochures, photos, web links and anything else that can provide you with information and visuals related to your client's business: This material will not only help keep your work targeted and relevant, it will also provide you with conceptual and visual cues for the creative tasks that lie ahead.

- Work with the client to come up with lists of words that you can take back to the studio for brainstorming sessions of your own. Come up with lists of nouns related to what your client produces as well as lists of adjectives related to positive aspects of their business. (Using words as brainstorm fuel is covered in depth beginning on page 17).

- Try to get a feel for any musts (if any) the client has in mind. For instance, the client might say that "The design must include the silhouette of a hummingbird," or, "The logo must be able to fit within wide horizontal

spaces," or, "The color chartreuse must not appear in the signature."

- Find out all you can about the client's target audience (special attention is given to this topic beginning on the next page).

- Discuss the client's competition (see page 15).

- Ask the client what kinds of logos they especially like, and also inquire about logos they don't like. These conversations may guide you toward paths of least resistance while also helping you avoid wasting time on impossible-to-sell ideas.

- Query the client about their color preferences. What colors do they love? What colors do they hate? Are they open to ideas? What colors do they think their target audience will respond to? What colors are their competition using?

- When meeting with the client, use your eyes as well as your ears to build a picture of their tastes and preferences. Does the decor and design of the client's office offer any insights? What about the art hanging on their walls? Do the clothes worn by the logo committee offer any clues as to their stylistic preferences? Do certain colors dominate the client's environment? Does anything you see lead to logo-related questions worth asking?

A tip: Logos are serious business for both the designer and the client. Take notes! Not only do notes give you solid reference material for later on, but the very act of

meticulously recording information and ideas on paper tends to impress clients and give them confidence in the thoroughness with which you will be approaching this all-important job.

Before your meeting with the client is concluded, spend time coming up with a brief consensus of what's been covered. With the client's help, produce two or three short sentences that sum up the project's goals. Not only will these sentences help keep your work targeted, they also can be used to give those who are present in the next meeting (the meeting where you return with your initial set of logo designs) an in-common frame of reference by which to evaluate your ideas.

WHO IT'S FOR

The logo you are about to design isn't for you. And really, it's not for the client, either. The logo you and your client will be developing is for the client's target audience. This is an extremely important distinction to keep in mind as you work, and the importance of accurately identifying—and getting inside the heads of—the people who might have an interest in what your client produces or does can't be understated.

- Ask your client to describe exactly who their target audience is. The majority of clients will have a clear answer to this question, but others might need the help of a marketing or focus-group study to accurately identify who their logo will be speaking to. Whatever

Take notes! Not only do notes give you solid reference material for later on, but the very act of meticulously recording information and ideas on paper tends to impress clients and give them confidence in the thoroughness with which you will be approaching this all-important job.

the case, it's essential that the client's target audience be identified and defined before work on the logo begins in earnest.

- Look into the media favored by the project's target audience. For instance, if you are working on a logo for a clothing company that specializes in young-teen fashion, then pick up some magazines that are popular with this crowd, investigate the TV programs and movies they watch, check out the ways their favorite musicians are marketed and visit the websites they love. Take note of the colors, typefaces, styles and content of their preferred media and try to do so without preconceived notions or assumptions: Unless you are currently a card-carrying member of the demographic group you're investigating, then what you think you know about these people stands a good chance of being a little—or entirely—misguided.

- If necessary, take the time to diplomatically talk with the client about the importance of putting their own tastes and preferences behind those of their target audience. (You may be surprised how many people have never really had a reason—until they take part in the creation of a logo for their business—to ponder the notion that the way they view the world may be quite a bit different than the way others see it.)

- What about attending an event where the target audience is likely to gather? A trade show, a conference,

The logo you are about to design isn't for you. And really, it's not for the client, either. The logo you and your client will be developing is for the client's target audience. This is an extremely important distinction to keep in mind as you work.

a sporting event, a concert or a rally? Observe and talk with the participants to get a better idea of the things that attract and hold their attention.

Have you got a handle on your client's expectations and wishes? Are you beginning to understand how the target audience sees things? Excellent. Now, if you haven't begun doing so already, there's still one more group of entities that you ought to investigate in order to properly prepare for the work ahead: the client's competition.

RIVALS

To ensure that the logo you create is notably different— and hopefully better—than what competitors are using, you'll need to look into two things: who the client's competition is, and what these competitors' logos and promotional materials look like.

- Ask your client for a list of competitors (rare is the client who won't have this kind of information memorized).

- Take a careful look at how these companies promote themselves. Assess the logos they use, the typefaces they favor, the images they feature, the styles they prefer, the colors they employ and anything else that conveys who the companies are and what they do.

- Once you are done researching the competition, make it a goal to create your client's logo in a way that is different, better looking and more thematically relevant than anything in use by their competitors.

THE POWER OF WORDS

See that image on the left? What's it an image of? If you answered, "a flower," you're absolutely right, and, chances are, if you asked a hundred people the same question, the vast majority would come up with the same answer.

Now, imagine taking another group of a hundred people, putting them in a large classroom with art supplies, writing the word *flower* on the chalkboard and asking each person to paint a picture of what that word means. Do you think any two people in the room would come up with exactly the same visual expression? The chances of that happening, even if a thousand people took part in the exercise, are remote at best.

Could it be that maybe—just maybe—the old saying, "A picture is worth a thousand words," has things backwards? At least in some cases? Isn't it time to acknowledge that words are as capable of launching pictures as vice versa, and also to give words a fair chance of proving their image-generating worth? The brainstorming stage of your next logo project would be the perfect place to give words just that opportunity.

Have you already met with the client and been brought up to speed regarding their tastes, goals and expectations? Have you researched what your client produces or does? Do you have the lists of brainstormed words and sentences from your first meeting in front of you? (These lists are described on page 11.) Have you

Could it be that maybe—just maybe—the old saying, "A picture is worth a thousand words," has things backwards? At least in some cases?

"FLOWER" = ✿ × 1000?

evaluated the preferences of the target audience and undertaken a thorough survey of the logos of competing businesses? Yes? Then now it's time to convert all of this material (and more) into lists of words capable of transforming themselves into thumbnail sketches and presentation-ready designs.

• Place yourself in front of a large piece of paper.

• Write down words from the lists of products, descriptors and goals that you and your client came up with during your initial meeting. Once the words have been written, use your brain and a thesaurus to expand the content of your lists into as many related words as possible.

• Next, come up with a list of the different ways and scenarios in which the client's product can be used. Do the same for any services it offers. Make another list of the ways in which a person could use the client's product or how people take advantage of their services.

• List words that describe symbolic material that relates positively to the client's business (the sun or a bird in flight, for example, as symbols of energy and freedom). This is a particularly important list: Very effective logos are often built around icons that express themselves in both symbolic and representational terms.

• Take your time making all of these lists. Use research material to expand your collection of words and consider brainstorming with others for more ideas: Know that the time spent populating your lists will streamline the upcoming search for visuals and con-

How can these lists of words and sentences be converted into logos? The answer to this question will emerge as soon as you start making the lists: Just try to stop the flow of ideas as certain words interact with your designer's mind to generate potentially useful ideas—ideas that could be applied to a logo's form, content or style of presentation.

veyances that can be used to establish the content and the look of the logos you are about to develop.

How can these lists of words and sentences be converted into logos? The answer to this question will emerge as soon as you start making the lists: Just try to stop the flow of ideas as certain words interact with your designer's mind to generate potentially useful ideas—ideas that could be applied to a logo's form, content or style of presentation.

• Allow single words from your lists to launch ideas.

• Consider the visual imagery that arises when words from various lists are combined—this is where things often get the most interesting and the most productive. For example, say you're working for a client called Sharp Tooth Music. You see the word *alligator* on your list of sharp-toothed animals, then you spy the word *piano* on your list of music-related terms, and the next thing you know, an image of a smiling alligator whose back is lined with piano keys springs to mind. Now it's your turn to smile: You've just come up with the first of several potentially winning logo ideas.

What's the best way of transforming your half-formed mental pictures and concepts into tangible visuals that can be evaluated, developed and—possibly—fine-tuned into presentation-ready material? Through thrifty little idea-saving sketches known as thumbnails.

19

Insist upon yourself. Be original.

Ralph Waldo Emerson

Only those with no memory insist on their originality.

Coco Chanel

Authenticity is invaluable; originality is non-existent.

In any case, always remember what

Jean-Luc Godard said: "It's not where you take

things from–it's where you take them to."

Jim Jarmusch

Some people believe in the possibility of true originality. Others believe that—in reality—it's been a long time since there was anything new under the sun. Still others believe that creativity is a matter of accepting that originality is impossible while simultaneously striving for truly meaningful work. One of these views could be 100 percent right, but it's probably more likely that all three contain truths that could be applied to the creative process. Take the project you are working on, for example. Should the logo you create appear unique and totally unlike the competition's? Yes, absolutely. Is it okay if your logo's style has been inspired or influenced by designs of a previous era (or by designs in this book, for that matter)? Sure, why not? Is it desirable to aim for clear conveyances of relevance and authentic meaning with every logo you create? Without a doubt.

THINKING BIG WITH LITTLE PICTURES

If, one day, you are assigned a logo project and immediately discover that the perfect, award-winning, client-pleasing and money-making solution has spontaneously materialized in your brain, then what you are probably experiencing is what is known as *your lucky day*—enjoy it and make a point of buying some lottery tickets before midnight.

During the far more typical days that lie ahead—the ones that are neither particularly lucky nor unlucky—know that the logos you are assigned will probably require a great deal of focused attention and concentrated effort along with a good measure of that old-fashioned thing usually described with the four letters: *w-o-r-k*.

If today is of the more typical variety, and you've already done the w-o-r-k necessary to give yourself a good grasp of the client's needs, the target audience's tastes and the competition's marketing strategies, and if you've already come up with (or are in the process of coming up with) the brainstorm-boosting lists mentioned on the previous pages, then it's time to start producing some visuals. And, as most successful designers would agree, the kinds of visuals you ought to be producing at this point are those quickly rendered idea-developing doodles and drawings known as thumbnail sketches.

Thumbnail sketches are beautiful things. Not so much in terms of how they look (many designers' thumbnail sketches are far from lovely) but in terms

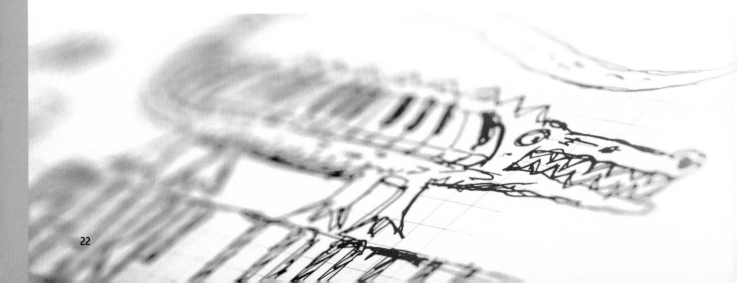

of what they can do. Thumbnails are quick sketches—usually small and roughly drawn—that act as a kind of visual shorthand to record and develop ideas that pop into designers' heads as they work.

- Concentrate on quantity more than quality when creating thumbnail sketches.

- Use large sheets of paper as a way of letting your brain and hand know that they can freely express themselves without wasting precious space.

- Refer to your brainstormed word lists constantly as you create thumbnail sketches. Often, the best ideas are the ones that arrive when a designer is prompted to consider unlikely associations between visuals and themes—or when they come across something that inspires them to make just the right modification or addition to a design.

- Keep an eye on any reference material you collected when researching your client's business. Allow these materials to spark ideas on their own and in conjunction with your word lists and thumbnail sketches.

- Use all kinds of visual material to further inspire and broaden your search for creative solutions. *The Logo Brainstorm Book* is an excellent sketch pad companion during the thumbnail stage of logo projects, as are design annuals and other sources of artistic and design-related inspiration.

- Dig deep: Create thumbnails until all the merely good ideas have been exhausted and then go further—into

Thumbnail sketches are beautiful things. Not so much in terms of how they look (many designers' thumbnail sketches are far from lovely) but in terms of what they can do. Thumbnails are quick sketches—usually small and roughly drawn—that act as a kind of visual shorthand to record and develop ideas that pop into designers' heads.

the realm of the great ideas. (Even the best designers regularly find themselves sketching several pages of ideas that look a lot like what the world has already seen before breaking into fresh creative territory.)

- Put maximum creative effort into your thumbnail sketches: The work done on paper at this point in a project stands a very good chance of improving—often greatly—the quality and efficiency of any computer-based work that follows.

- How much time should be spent on thumbnail sketches? How many should you do? Naturally, the answers to questions like these depend on a lot of things: your creative stamina, the project's deadline, gut feelings, etc. In general, however, know that it's best to keep at it until

you are nothing short of wildly ecstatic over at least as many ideas as you are planning to present to the client.

PREPARING FOR PRESENTATION

Not so many years ago, logo ideas were initially presented to clients in the form of tightly executed renderings called "comps" (short for "comprehensive roughs"). Most of the time, comps were drawn using felt markers, straightedges, french curves and ellipse guides. Comps were illustrated far more precisely than thumbnail sketches, but, at the same time, they were rarely meant to come across as finished designs (keep in mind that every letter of a logo presented in this way had to be rendered by hand—and it's no easy task to depict any type-

These days, because software has made it possible to spend less time creating picture-perfect artwork than it used to take to render even a rough comp, designers are expected to present their logo ideas as highly polished and nearly finalized designs.

face's characters with absolute accuracy). One nice thing about comps was that their inherent not-quite-finalized look allowed viewers to consider them with some conceptual and aesthetic breathing room—as though the designs expressed themselves by saying, "This is pretty much the idea, but, as you can see, the final beautifying will take place later on, so don't worry about the smaller details for now."

Computers have changed all that. These days, because software has made it possible to spend less time creating picture-perfect artwork than it used to take to render even a rough comp, designers are expected to present their logo ideas as highly polished and nearly finalized designs.

Are you ready to turn your selected thumbnail sketches into presentable visuals? If so, then unless you are producing one of those increasingly rare logos that is rendered using pencils, pens or brushes, it's time to turn on the computer and to launch some software.

- As you work using the computer, keep your thumbnail sketches nearby and refer to the drawings often. Strive to retain the creative essence of your spontaneously created sketches as you translate them into computer-generated logo designs.

- If you are working on a relatively complex creation (or one that includes elements that have distinctly hand-rendered qualities) and have developed a tight thumbnail sketch of the idea, consider scanning the

sketch and importing it into the computer for use as a traceable guide.

- Does the logo you are working on include both typography and an icon? If so, then consider developing the design's icon first. Many designers prefer this order of business since the visual personality of a fully developed icon can set the tone for any typographic and decorative elements that are added later. (That said, if there is a typeface that you definitely want to use for a particular logo, then by all means, allow the font to play the role of theme-setter for that signature.)

- Be willing to explore your options when adding typography to any design. Consider fonts that are likely to be successful, as well as typefaces that seem like long

shots: It's not at all uncommon for a designer to fall in love with a typographic solution that wasn't even in the running during the early stages of a logo's development.

- Use this book's many type-plus-icon samples—as well as its type-only designs—to help brainstorm for ways of selecting typefaces and presenting words as part of a logo design.

- Take advantage of the versatility of software and thoroughly explore compositional variables between your logo's elements. It's rare to be gifted with a crystal-clear picture of what it is you are trying to create at the beginning of a logo project. Always work toward what you believe is the ideal outcome, and also keep your mind perpetually open to adjustments,

revisions and even radical changes as your logo's form moves from inception to finalization.

- When you have developed a design that seems especially promising, save it, make a copy of it and then explore some options: Try out alternative typographic approaches, different compositional details and a variety of finishing touches. This is a very important stage of the creative process. It's amazing how often a design that initially appeared wonderful suddenly looks incomplete and unexciting when compared with a later incarnation.

- Critique your logos in a thorough and fair way before showing them to the client. Try this: Print your logo on a letter-sized sheet of paper, tack or tape it to a wall, take a short break outside the room and then return and evaluate the design from several paces away. This simple routine helps clear designers' brains before offering their eyes a fresh vantage point from which to critique their work.

- How about inviting one or more coworkers to join you in the critiquing process?

How will you know when your logo design is ready to show to the client? When nothing can be added or taken away to improve its visual appeal, when its thematic conveyances are perfectly in tune with the goals of the project and when your trustworthy design-sense feels fully satisfied with every aspect of your creation.

Print your logo on a letter-sized sheet of paper, tack or tape it to a wall, take a short break outside the room and then return and evaluate the design from several paces away. This simple routine helps clear designers' brains before offering their eyes a fresh vantage point from which to critique their work.

2 Symbols

CHAPTER CONTENTS

2   Symbols

SYMBOLS ARE VISUAL SHORTHAND—pictorial abbreviations for creatures, places, things, expressions and ideas. Companies and organizations often include a symbol as part of their signature (another word for logo). An effective symbol snares the attention of its target audience in a positive way and bolsters the image of the company it stands for.

Does every company need to be represented by a signature that includes a symbol (as opposed to going with a purely typography signature)? No, but certain benefits do arise when a company includes an abstract or pictorial icon as part of its logo. For one thing, studies have shown that a company's icon can be

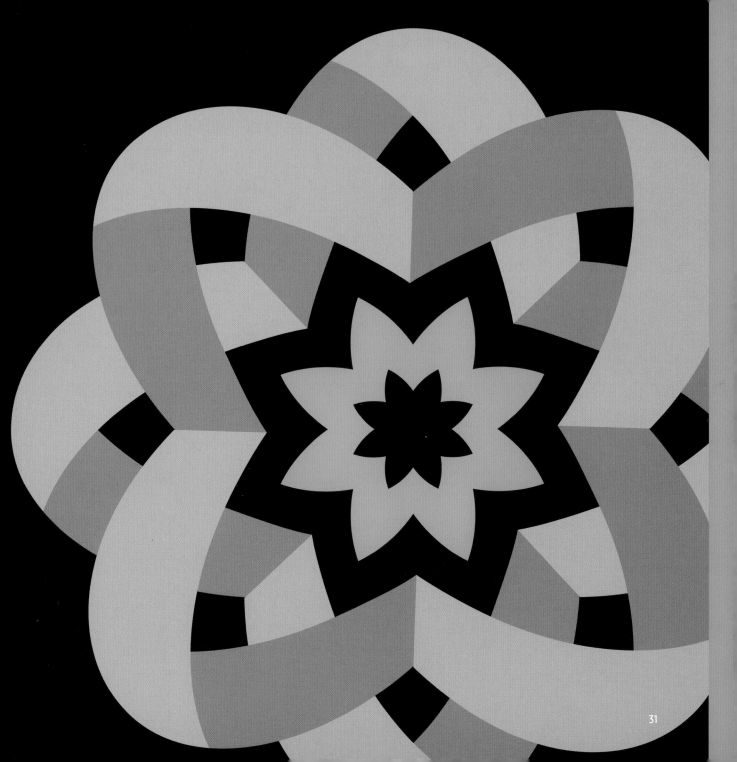

recognized far more quickly than its typographically rendered name. Also, a company's icon—once it has become familiar to its audience—can be used to personify a company without the help of type (Nike's swoosh is a good example of an icon that is able to perform its duties without typographic assistance).

If you haven't done so already, now would be an excellent time to read this book's introduction (pages 1–3) and its first chapter (Beginnings, pages 4–27). These sections describe the importance and the how-tos of gaining an understanding of the client's expectations and the tastes of the target audience before beginning a logo project. The intro and first chapter also offer suggestions about getting ideas flowing once you have established a sense for where the project is heading.

The following pages are meant to aid the process of producing effective and attractive symbols. Take a look at the chapters ahead if you'd like to explore type-based icons (also known as monograms), if you want to investigate type-only logos, if you want help brainstorming for ways of combining symbols with type, if you are thinking about combining symbolic and typographic elements into emblem-like structures or if you are seeking eye-catching and timely color combinations for any kind of signature design.

Expansive thinking

In terms of possibilities, the seventeen variations of the square shown on this spread are just the tip of the iceberg. In fact, compared with the number of ways in which the essence of a square can be visually portrayed, these designs are not even the tip of the atom on the sharpest dendrite* of the tiniest snowflake at the edge of the most remote iceberg in Antarctica. *Infinite*—that's how many different ways there are to visually interpret any shape, object, theme or concept. This is very good news for designers because it means that there are a whole lot of potential solutions for any logo project, and all that needs to be done is to develop three or four of these possibilities into presentation-worthy designs.

Take the lesson illustrated here to heart: If a shape as simple as a square can be so readily converted into such a wide range of interpretations, imagine what could be done with the much more intricate and interesting subject matter you'll be dealing with on your next logo project.

*A dendrite *is the star-like crystal and its delicate side branches that define the structure of a snowflake. How about using that one in a sentence the next time you're walking in a snowstorm with a friend?*

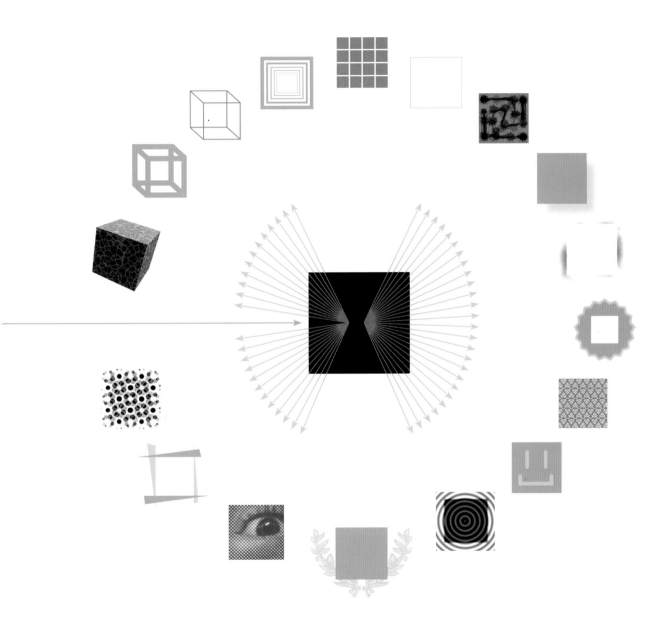

Building icons from basic shapes

An excellent place to begin the search for a non-representational symbol design is through associations between basic shapes. The familiar geometric forms of circles, squares, triangles and ellipses can be merged, trimmed, warped, intersected, multiplied or divided in order to create simple icons that are capable of delivering complex connotations in eye-catching ways.

On this spread, basic geometric forms have been used to build a varied series of icons. Use these samples—as well as those featured throughout *The Logo Brainstorm Book*—to prompt avenues of exploration as you brainstorm for logo solutions. And remember, all of this book's samples are intended as mere starting points for creative discovery: If you see an idea that appeals to you, register the idea in your mind and then let your own preferences, ideas and goals lead you wherever they will.

[A] A simple arrangement of line-rendered squares. Investigate your options whenever you are developing a linework-based design (see pages 54–55 for ideas). **[B–D]** Patterns built by rotating solid and translucent shapes around a center point. **[E]** A symbol created using several different weights of line, multiple colors and a variety of Adobe Illustrator's transparency effects. **[F]** How about a free-form collection of shapes? What about wrapping your geometric forms with ultra-thick borders? **[G]** Would extreme horizontal proportions suit the project you are working on? Illustrator's Gradient panel was used to fill this pattern of overlapping diamonds with a radial blend of colors. **[H,I]** Designs made from multiple copies of a shape. Explore patterns built from shapes of the same size, as well as arrangements made from shapes of various sizes and proportions. **[J]** Contrast is the goal here: A crisply rendered star has been placed over top of a hand-painted circle. **[K]** Elliptical holes have been punched through the forms of a pair of colored triangles to create this sideways-pointing icon.

A

B

C

D

E

F

G

H

I

J

K

Adding dimension

The samples on this spread are dimensional variations of the designs featured on the previous page. Would suggestions of depth add to the appeal of an icon you're working on?

On a technical note, it's worth mentioning that the 3-D renderings in samples **A, C** and **G** were made using a free, open-source program called Blender. Interested in creating abstract or representational icons of this kind? Consider giving Blender or another 3-D program a try. Be advised that these programs operate much differently than vector-based software, and even if you're a proficient Illustrator or Photoshop user, you'll probably experience a steep learning curve as you enter the realm of multi-dimensional software. Stick with it, though: Even a basic understanding of 3-D software will allow you to have fun with this technology while enabling you to produce intriguing and attractive designs.

[A] A 3-D rendering program was used to create this dimensional interpretation of a formation of cubes. One of the many convenient features of 3-D software is its capability of moving a virtual camera around a scene in search of the best view of an object. **[B]** A symbol drawn in isometric perspective using Illustrator's vector-based tools. **[C]** Transparency and lighting effects available through 3-D software were employed to render this symmetrical arrangement of translucent forms. **[D]** How about using Illustrator's Gradient panel to shade flat geometric shapes in a way that implies solidity and depth? **[E]** A simple arrangement of lines and circles have established the perspective-implying appearance of this icon. **[F]** Drop shadows lift the forms of these four basic shapes off the page and apart from each other. **[G]** A pattern of dimensional diamonds built, warped, bent, tilted and lit using 3-D software. **[H]** Illustrator's perspective controls were used to visually swell a pattern of dots from the previous page into this depth-conveying symbol. **[I]** What about adding an implication of dimension through subtle black extensions? **[J]** Conveyances of depth are achieved by allowing parts of this icon's star to rise above—and other parts to sink below—the translucent circle that encloses it. **[K]** This design's perspective-obeying shadow was made from a copy of the icon itself: Photoshop tools were used to re-proportion, blur and recolor the shadow.

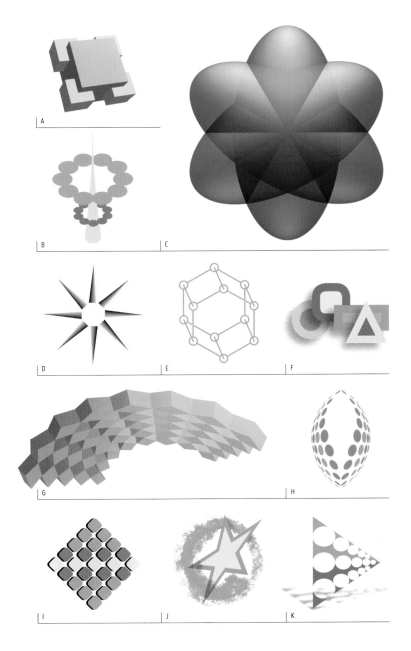

A

B

C

D

E

F

G

H

I

J

K

Simple beginnings, complex finishes

As few as one or two basic shapes can be repeated, rotated, resized, warped, overlapped, repositioned, changed in color or given different levels of opacity to produce all kinds of complex and intriguing symbols. This spread features two such designs: A multidimensional creation built from copies of a single sphere and a 2-D design made from a variety of circles. Would an elaborate creation such as these suit the project you are working on? How complex could your design be? Over-the-top or merely to the edge of reason? When creating an intricate visual, be mindful of how the icon will be used: Avoid designs that will not render clearly when presented at smaller sizes.

Visual arithmetic

Computers allow designers of today to explore a great deal more creative territory per hour than designers of the ink-and-paper era were able to cover in twice the time.

Among the gifts that software has granted computer-using designers are virtual tools that can be used to quickly investigate the outcomes of mergers, subtractions and intersections between geometric and free-form shapes. PATHFINDER operations (available through Adobe Illustrator and InDesign) were employed to generate the symbols featured on the opposite page using only squares and circles as building material.

[A] A symmetrical design built by applying PATHFINDER operations to circles. **[B]** A not-quite-symmetrical symbol made entirely from rectangles. **[C]** PATHFINDER operations were applied to squares and ellipses to create the components of this upwardly expressive design. **[D–L]** Nine icons that were each created using only circles and PATHFINDER operations. Interested in experimenting with the PATHFINDER panel? Try starting out with circles and ellipses—shapes that have an almost uncanny tendency to produce aesthetically pleasing results when combined, subtracted or merged. **[M]** How about creating an icon from a quilt-like pattern of shapes? Quilted patterns are often made from combinations of simple geometric forms. **[N]** A design based entirely on additions and subtractions between squares. **[O]** The reversed form of a square sits at the center of this set of overlapping arcs. **[P]** Circles were used to carve corners from this design's joined rectangles.

Illustrator's PATHFINDER panel and its action-generating buttons and menus. InDesign offers PATHFINDER commands through its Object pull-down menu.

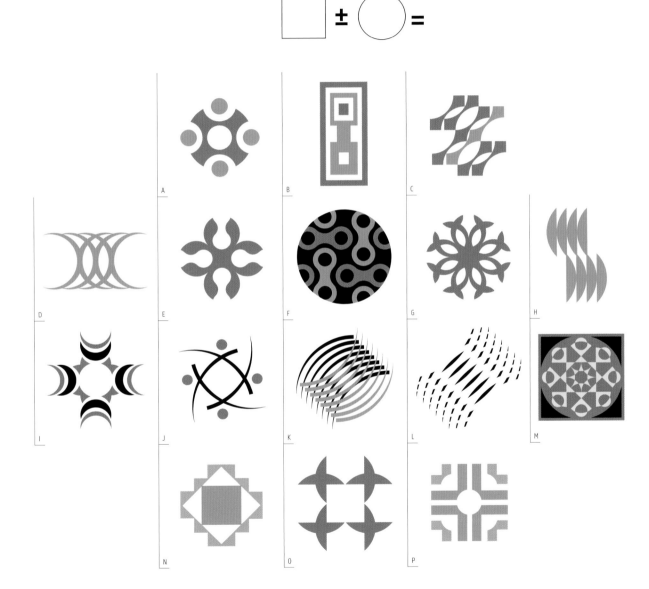

More shapes, more visual math

This spread features a collection of symbols created by applying PATHFINDER operations—along with rotation, transformation and repetition treatments—to one or more basic shapes. The results range from simple to complex, precise to casual, symmetrical to free-form.

Many designers find that PATHFINDER tools are best explored through hands-on experience (as opposed to spending excessive time with the Help menu or the users' manual). If you are unfamiliar with the way PATHFINDER operations work, try this: Open a new document in Illustrator, create an assortment of basic shapes along the outer edges of the workspace (this will leave the center of the document clear for your upcoming creations), open the PATHFINDER panel using the Window menu, drag copies of two or more shapes to the center of the workspace,

overlap their forms and start clicking the PATHFINDER panel's buttons and seeing what happens. Try out each of the panel's buttons and menu commands, see what happens when shapes are stacked in different orders, apply PATHFINDER operations to combinations of your basic shapes and to the results of previous operations, consider applying transformation treatments (scaling, skewing, rotating, duplicating, etc.) as you work and feel free to explore the offerings of Illustrator's Effect menu. Anything goes here: The goal is to enjoy some unstructured creative playtime while acquainting yourself with the capabilities of one of Illustrator's most powerful set of tools. (And be sure to save any clever-looking designs you come up with—one of your creations just might fit the needs of a future design project.)

Anyone who has never made a mistake has never tried anything new.

Albert Einstein

A computer lets you make more mistakes faster than any other invention ... with the possible exceptions of handguns and tequila.

Mitch Ratcliffe

You probably know something about Babe Ruth's long-standing home run record, but did you also know that he struck out more times than any other player of his era? Did The Babe's propensity for striking out ever dampen his zeal for hitting baseballs out of the park? Not a bit. "Never let the fear of striking out keep you from playing the game," was all he had to say on the matter. How about applying this attitude to your logo work? Make a point of accepting the inevitable misses, false starts and dead ends that will occur as you develop concepts for presentation. After all, the computer's "undo" command makes it easier than ever to move beyond ideas that are missing the mark and to take a fresh swing at scoring a winner.

Combining dimensional shapes

How about using dimensional shapes to build an abstract or a representational icon? If you are adept with 3-D software, then you know that it can be used to stack, layer, rotate and merge shapes of any description in accordance with—or in defiance of—real-world physics. This makes dimensional media a fun tool for artists who want to mimic perceptions of reality, as well as for those who want to create reality-bending designs.

Dimensional symbols and illustrations can also be created by hand or by using the drawing and perspective-conveying tools and effects offered through Photoshop and Illustrator's vector- and pixel-based tools.

Whether you plan on using 3-D software, or a program like Photoshop or Illustrator to construct a dimensional design, it's usually best to begin your work with pen-and-paper sketches. That way, you'll have visual guides to help direct and focus your efforts once you turn on the computer.

[A] Graduated shading and a subtle weaving of forms lend this trio of cogs a look of dimension and conveyances of connection. [B] Traditional-style building blocks presented in a futuristic manner: Past and present converge in this free-floating sculpture of carved wood. This icon's dimensional shapes were created using PATHFINDER-like operations offered through a 3-D program. [C] Working on a logo for a forward-thinking client? What about creating a depiction of a futuristic rocket, vehicle or plane? How about a robotic human hand or an android-like figure? What other objects or creatures from the future could you render as part of a logo? [D] A hovering dimensional diagram created with Illustrator's PEN tool and its PATHFINDER operations. The icon's curving arrow adds a sense of movement and connotations of before-and-after to the design.

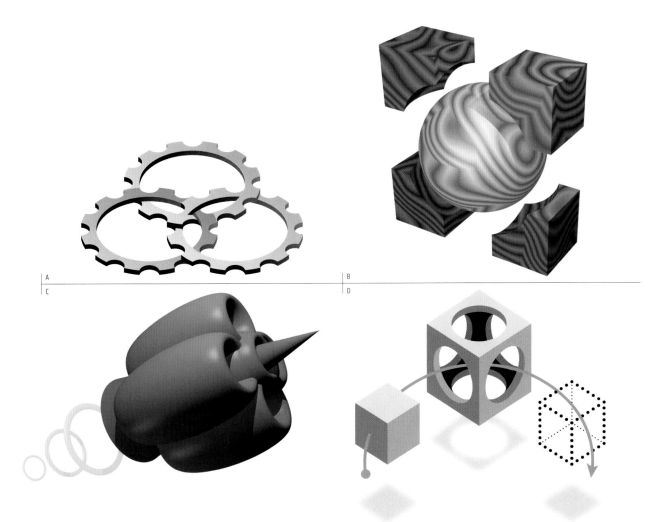

A   B

C   D

Free-form constructions

How about building an icon from one or more free-form shapes? The symbols on the opposite page have mostly been built from shapes that are neither rectangular, elliptical or triangular.

As with any icon-creation project, consider beginning your search for free-form symbol ideas by making lists of nouns and adjectives that could be converted into visual material, as well as by doing numerous thumbnail sketches of potential solutions. See chapter 1, Beginnings, pages 4–27, for more about initiating projects with brainstorming aids such as these.

[A–E] Five designs built from the free-form shape featured below. The shape has been flipped, angled, rotated, spun, overlapped and merged to create these outcomes. [F] Would strongly horizontal proportions work best for your client's logo applications? [G] The computer is not the only tool that can be used to produce icons: The bottoms of ceramic mugs—wetted with coffee and pressed against paper—produced this multi-ringed design. [H] PATHFINDER operations were used to create the components of this ornate symbol. [I,J] Consider lending your icon an informal tone by manually messing with the precise forms of its computer-generated shapes. [K] The expressive conveyances of this icon's free-form elements are amplified through the contrast provided by its precisely rendered backdrop. [L] What about creating a custom interpretation of a familiar symbol for use as a logo?

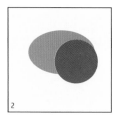

Illustrator's PATHFINDER operations are ideally suited for transforming basic geometric forms into free-form shapes. PATHFINDER's "Minus" operation is applied twice in the sequence above. [1] A circle and an ellipse are created. [2] The circle is positioned on top of the ellipse. [3] "Minus" is chosen from Illustrator's PATHFINDER panel to create a secondary shape. [4] A second circle is drawn and positioned over the free-form shape. [5] Illustrator's "Minus" option is used to subtract the form of the top circle from the bottom shape in order to produce a free-form arch. At this point, the arch could be used as a finished icon, or, as seen in the first five samples on the opposite page, it could be employed as a component of a more complex design.

A

B

C

D

E

F

G

H

I

J

K

L

Dimensional free-form constructions

What about coming up with a dimension-conveying free-form design for use as an icon? Logos like these can be created by hand, through programs like Photoshop or Illustrator or with the help of 3-D software.

Some of the samples on the opposite page have been shaded in ways that project illusions of depth, while others rely solely on perspective-implying shapes to convey dimension. Drop shadows have also been employed in two of the samples to lift those visuals from the page. Keep an eye out for different ways in which illustrators and designers add feelings of depth to two-dimensional artwork; experiment with a variety of approaches before deciding which is best for the design you are working on.

[A] A design made from repetitions of a single arch. Illustrator was used to repeat, skew and stretch copies of the arch to produce this depth-conveying icon. **[B]** Light drop shadows and subtle graduated shading are all that separate the white petals of this design from the page. **[C]** No shading, no drop shadows—just the illusion of depth created by a pair of overlapping, perspective-implying free-form shapes. **[D]** What about a more casual illustrative approach? And how about including a directional element such as an arrow in your symbol? **[E]** Here, a soft-edged cast shadow amplifies the dimensional presentation of a gently falling sheet of paper. **[F]** Know how to use 3-D software? Even a basic knowledge will allow you to create intriguing combinations of free-form shapes.

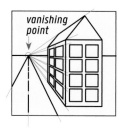

Ever hear of a vanishing point? A vanishing point is the spot at which parallel lines from the real world converge in a two-dimensional image. Artists who use pencils, paint and rulers to create dimensional illustrations often employ one, two or three (and sometimes more) vanishing points to build their compositions. An understanding of vanishing points and other principles of visual perspective can be useful to graphic designers as well—particularly when it comes to creating dimensional illustrations and logos. If you want to learn more about conveying illusions of depth through two-dimensional media, search the Web, art stores, bookstores and libraries for how-to information.

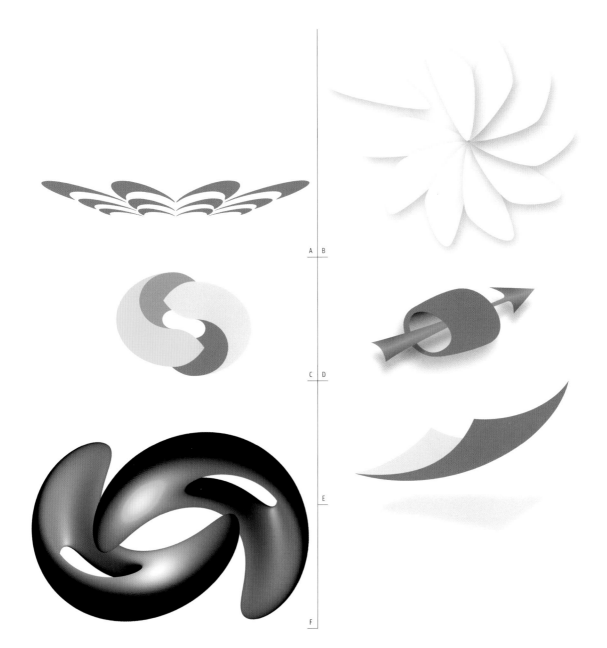

A B

C D

E

F

53

Linework

Twenty-five semi-abstract renderings of a transmission tower—each created using some form of linework—are presented on the opposite page. Use this spread to help generate ideas when you are working on an abstract or a representational symbol that is being constructed with lines of one or more weight or style.

When using the computer to create linework-based designs, it's very easy to try out different weights, styles, caps (the rounded, squared or shaped endpoints of lines) and joints (rounded or square bends) before deciding what produces the most effective result. Software can also be used to create lines that appear to have been drawn with real-world tools like pencils, pens and brushes. (And don't forget that actual pencils, pens and brushes are always an option worth considering when deciding how to render linework.)

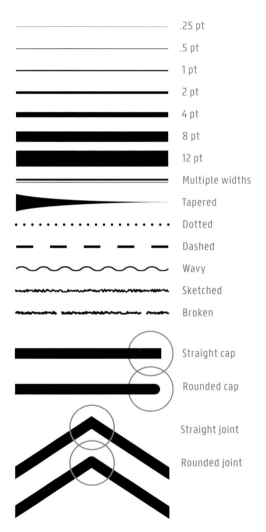

.25 pt
.5 pt
1 pt
2 pt
4 pt
8 pt
12 pt
Multiple widths
Tapered
Dotted
Dashed
Wavy
Sketched
Broken
Straight cap
Rounded cap
Straight joint
Rounded joint

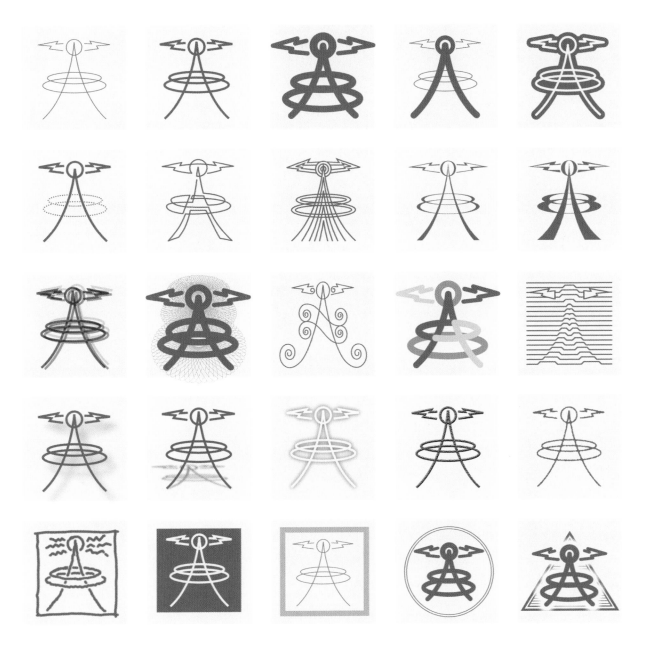

Reinterpreting reality

This is what designers do: They come up with attractive and engaging ways of depicting things, people, places, feelings, expressions, actions and ideas. The visuals designers create arise from a mix of skills, personal preferences, the wishes of the client and the tastes of the target audience. The rest of this chapter is devoted to aiding designers in the work of searching for effective renderings of tangible things and their intangible conveyances. Take a look at the interpretations of the coffee cup shown opposite. See anything there that sparks an idea that could be applied to the logo you are working on? What about the samples on the next spread, or on the pages after that?

Depicting with basic shapes

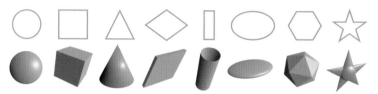

The first half of this chapter featured abstract icons made from simple geometric forms. Representational symbols, too, can be fashioned from basic shapes. Depictions of creatures, places and things can be built using only circles, squares, triangles and/or ellipses. Illustrator's PATHFINDER operations can be employed to create components for both minimalist and complex renderings. 3-D software can also be used to create dimensional icons of real or imaginary subjects.

[A] A sunset scene built entirely from circles and rectangles. [B–D] How about using software to create a cyber-like depiction of one of nature's organic creations? [E,F] Simplified graphic depictions of laurels and leaves. These designs were built from PATHFINDER operations that were applied to ellipses. [G] Explore ideas that involve contrasting styles and forms. Here, an ornate swirl fills the silhouettes of a geometrically rendered stand of trees. [H,I] Consider rendering your subject in a highly simplified way. These icons were created using only circles and lines. [J] What about creating an icon that reflects the look of civic signage or international symbology? [K] Illustrator, InDesign and Photoshop offer a wide range of transparency effects that can be used to add a subtle sense of dimension to an icon. [L] Spheres, rods, ellipses and tori were assembled using 3-D software to create this futuristic vehicle. (The vehicle's circular backdrop and its shaded "zoom lines" were added in Photoshop.) [M] Decorative swirls contrast playfully with the geometrically rendered shapes of this design's subjects.

Use the Web, libraries and bookstores to search for reference material related to your subject matter when working on representational icons—especially when your goal is to accurately portray the form and essence of the creature, place or thing you're rendering.

A

B

C

D

E

F

G

H

I

J

K

L

M

59

Illustrating with PATHFINDER operations

Concise, detailed and elegant representational logos can be rendered using PATHFINDER operations. Components in each of the designs on the facing page were made by applying a sequence of PATHFINDER operations that began with interactions between two or more basic shapes.

It's worth noting, too, that all but one of the icons were created—entirely or in part—by applying PATHFINDER operations to ellipses of various sizes and proportions. The natural beauty of ellipses (along with their ability to convey the appearance of a circle seen in perspective) make them ideally suited as building material for both abstract and representational icons created with PATHFINDER tools.

A suggestion: Don't skip the thumbnail phase when creating these kinds of icons. Your sketches need not be tightly rendered or particularly accurate—their only purpose is to identify a range of possible solutions and to offer a sense of direction for the computer-based work that will follow. (See page 22 for more about thumbnail sketches.)

[A] Simple icons featuring concise renderings of everyday objects can be created using Illustrator's PATHFINDER operations. [B] This symbol's needle was created using PATHFINDER operations; its ornate swirl of thread was made by joining segments cut from ellipses. [C] Simple shapes shaded simply define the form of this skyward-pointing paper airplane. [D] An icon made from a pair of opposing strips of film rendered using PATHFINDER operations. (Interestingly, depictions of film remain suitable material for icons related to photography and cinema even though digital media has largely made film a thing of the past.) [E] An open book, also created using PATHFINDER operations. Advice: A tight thumbnail sketch created in advance will speed your work once you begin finalizing a design with the computer. [F] A detailed and graphically rendered trio of fir cones—created through repetitions of just one free-form shape and a single arch. [G] A symmetrical and unambiguous depiction of a torch topped by an expressively abstract flame. How about infusing your icon's visual personality with suggestions of thematic complexity by illustrating its components with contrasting styles? [H] Connotations of movement are added to this hummingbird's static form through the repeated and multicolored shapes that define its wings.

A
B
C
D
E
F
G
H

Contextual collisions

Anything look familiar? Why have some of the stand-alone icons from the previous page been paired in order to produce these designs? It's to make a point: Always keep in mind the theme-generating and intrigue-building potential that occurs when two or more seemingly disconnected visuals are combined into one. Use the word-list brain-storming practices described on pages 17–19 to help produce a range of material for consideration when aiming for icons of this kind.

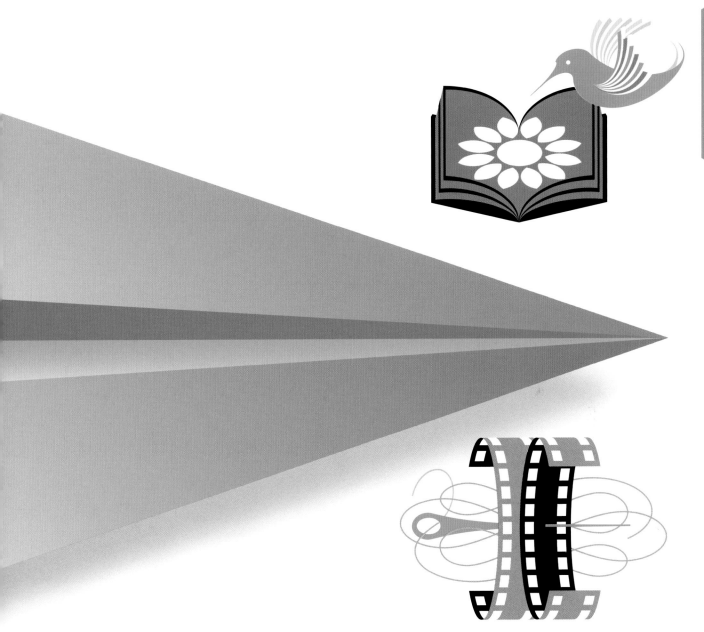

The artist is a collector of things imaginary or real. He accumulates things with the same enthusiasm that a little boy stuffs his pockets. The scrap heap and the museum are embraced with equal curiosity.

Paul Rand (from *A Designer's Art*)

Ideas come from everything.

Alfred Hitchcock

Want to drive your car across town? Put some gas in its tank. Need to turn on a lamp? Plug it in. And what about your brain? Is it fueled and plugged in? One thing is for sure, the graphic designers who consistently produce top-level work are the same ones who can continually be seen doing things like reading, watching movies, listening to new and old music, walking around attentively, having conversations with friends and strangers and getting their hands dirty in the garden: whatever connects them to—and informs them about—life and living. What do they do with the impressions and information that comes from these experiences? For one thing, they convert them into eye-catching and communicative logos.

Degrees of simplification

The ibex is an extraordinarily agile and pow-erful creature that inhabits some of the most rugged and inhospitable terrain on earth. Char-acterized by a magnificent set of spiraling horns and a generous beard, the ibex is certainly one of the more aesthetically intriguing animals on earth. Here, it is used to demonstrate three answers to a question that designers must ask themselves every time they create a representational icon: To what degree should I simplify the form of my subject in order to come up with an effective and attractive icon?

Naturally, there is no "right" answer to this question: It's up to you, the designer, to decide how to go about converting a real-life creature or thing into a graphic icon, and the samples at right—along with each of this chapter's representational symbols—are offered as visual prompts to help you brainstorm your way to a potent and compelling solution.

[A] An ibex that has been minimally rendered using a continuous line and two tiny ellipses. The animal's beard has been omitted from this design and the next—its distinctive set of horns being the ele-ment that has been singled out as the icons' main descriptive feature. Tough decisions often have to be made about what to leave in and what to leave out when crafting a simplified icon of any creature, place or thing. [B] Gracefully tapered and boldly rendered, the sweeping elliptical horns of this graphically rendered ibex deliver forceful connota-tions of strength and elegance. The sharply cut eye indents lend a pleasing note of contrast to a design built mostly from curves. [C] One step closer to realism. Details of this design have been crafted to closely replicate the visual nature of the animal's features—the shape of its eyes, the fold of its ears, the texture of its horns and the form of its nostrils. Less accurately rendered is the ibex's beard: Artis-tic license was called upon to depict this aspect of the goat's facade in a more visually capricious style.

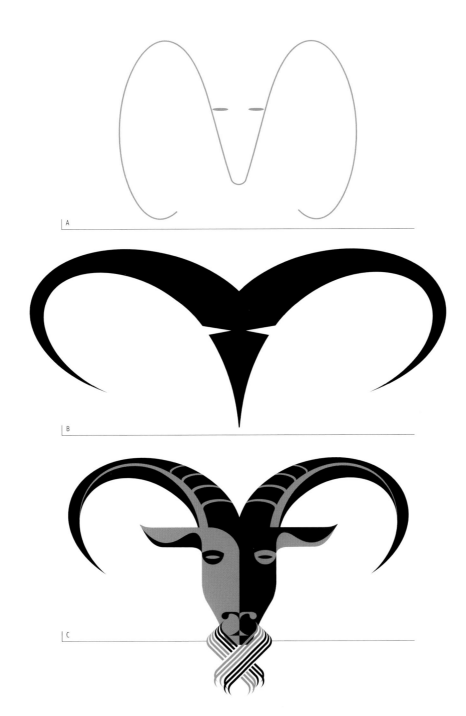

A

B

C

Graphic interpretations

When developing a representational icon, the degree to which the person, animal, place or thing is to be simplified must always be considered in tandem with the style in which it's to be portrayed. If the manner in which icons portray real-life creatures and things could be conveyed mathematically, the equation might look something like this:

$$Simplification \times Style = Graphic\ Interpretation$$

Each of the icons on the opposite page could be seen as products of this virtual equation. The icons have been arranged vertically according to subject (bees above globes above light bulbs) and horizontally according to the complexity of their rendering (simple on the left, complex to the right). A variety of stylistic approaches are scattered throughout the samples.

[A,B] Extreme simplicity: Straightforward graphic representations built from lines and basic shapes. [C] Conveyances of grace and elegance are brought into this design through stylishly tapered lines and free-form shapes. [D] What about creating an icon using silhouettes? And how about bending the definition of a silhouette by including translucent elements and hints of color? [E] Connotations of connection and purpose have been introduced into this symbol thorough the interaction between its components. [F] Night and day on earth—rendered using basic shapes and simple linework. [G] Tapered latitude lines that transition from black to white—and a curved demarcation between green and black portions of the globe—add notes of sophistication to this design. [H] This globe's lines of latitude also serve as indicators of motion. [I] A more complete grid of latitudinal and longitudinal markings—rendered in perspective using multiple weights of line—lend feelings of accuracy and an enhanced impression of dimension to this symbol. [J] What about an icon that embraces realism and embellishment on more or less equal terms? [K] Minimal, stylish and cleverly constructed: a visual approach that never seems to go out of style. [L] The starburst in this symbol imparts inferences of action and function to an otherwise static portrayal of a light bulb. [M] Light radiates from this icon in the form of outward-pointing pyramids of dots. Stylized reflections have been added to the bulb and its base to convey suggestions of depth and realism. [N] A case of casual precision: an icon built from the overlapping forms of precisely drawn elliptical arcs and misaligned shading. [O] How about taking things a step further and creating an over-the-top eyeful of overlapping lines and shapes?

A

B

C

D

E

F

G

H

I

J

K

L

M

N

O

Personality traits

Just as appearance and personality play major roles in terms of how a person is judged, these same factors go a long way in establishing how a logo is perceived.

How should your icon's conveyances of aesthetic quality and thematic personality be delivered to its target audience? Will it be through the simplicity of the icon's presentation? Through ornamentation and adornment? Through a casual, playful, serious or retro style of rendering? Will it be through a look that is extroverted and in-your-face or will it be through subdued implications of charisma?

Take a look at the icons on this spread. See anything that gives you ideas about how to best establish the graphic demeanor of the logo you're developing?

[A] A book with wings, depicted through lines and color. **[B]** Linked, locked and tilted—a symbol that generates a sense of unity and action. **[C]** Wings … or are they hands? An uplifting design with human conveyances. **[D]** Abstract and expressive: a decorative icon made from stacked and re-proportioned repetitions of a single tapered curve. **[E]** Strong yet delicate, bold yet decorative: a star-studded pair of wide-spread wings with a multifaceted visual personality. **[F]** A modern interpretation of a phoenix and its fiery wings make for an eye-catching symbol of renewal and vitality. **[G]** Curving, paper-like wings lift this pencil from the page. **[H]** A delicately drawn wing springs from a forward-gesturing treble clef. The tinted square behind the clef lends a note of structure to the otherwise free-form design while directing attention to the icon's focal point. **[I]** How about creating a custom-made monogram by replacing part of a letter with a visual component? (For more ideas along these lines, see pages 140–141.) **[J]** The look of this five-string banjo is made mythical by bracketing it between a pair of angelic wings and placing it over a starburst backdrop.

At left is an outline view of sample **[E]**. Each shape of the ornate wings was created using ellipses: The design's solid shapes were created by applying PATHFINDER operations to two or more overlapping ellipses; the curling lines were created by joining segments of two or more line-rendered ellipses.

A

B

C

D

E

F

G

H

I

J

Digital makeovers

The wing theme from the previous page continues on this spread, only here, one set of wings has been used to demonstrate a number of digital makeovers. Treatments and effects from both Illustrator and Photoshop were applied to the pair of wings shown above in order to produce the outcomes on the opposite page.

Unfamiliar with the treatments and effects offered through Illustrator and Photoshop? There's no better way to become acquainted with them than through hands-on experience: Locate a favorite illustration or photo on your hard drive, open it in Illustrator or Photoshop and start exploring the capabilities of the programs' filters, effects and transformation tools. Do this regularly—for work and for play—and it won't be long before you have a solid idea of which tools can be used to produce what kinds of results.

Illustrator and Photoshop notes:
[A] The SYMBOL SPRAYER tool has been used to fill this design with visual texture. (Illustrator) **[B]** The dappled fill inside these wings was created with the Difference Clouds filter. The design's edges were softened with blur tools. (Photoshop) **[C]** An illustrated pattern of colors was copied into this design using the Paste Into command. (Photoshop or Illustrator) **[D]** The Blur > Zoom filter has been applied to this set of wings. An unaltered copy of the original design was then pasted in front, colored white and made translucent. (Photoshop or Illustrator) **[E]** Transformation controls were used to create this re-proportioned incarnation of the design. (Photoshop or Illustrator) **[F]** The interior of these wings has been given a new look with the Chrome filter. The Outer Glow effect was used to add an orange glow around the design. (Photoshop or Illustrator) **[G]** This set of wings has been radically reshaped using the settings offered through the Pucker & Bloat filter. (Photoshop or Illustrator) **[H]** The Difference Clouds effect was applied to these wings and the Halftone Filter effect was aimed at the result. The orange fade around the design was added using the Outer Glow effect. (Photoshop or Illustrator) **[I]** A set of white wings has been placed in front of an intricate and toothy border. The border was created by applying the Zig Zag filter to the original design. (Photoshop or Illustrator) **[J]** The Grain filter was applied to the wings from sample **[B]** to produce this outcome. (Photoshop or Illustrator)

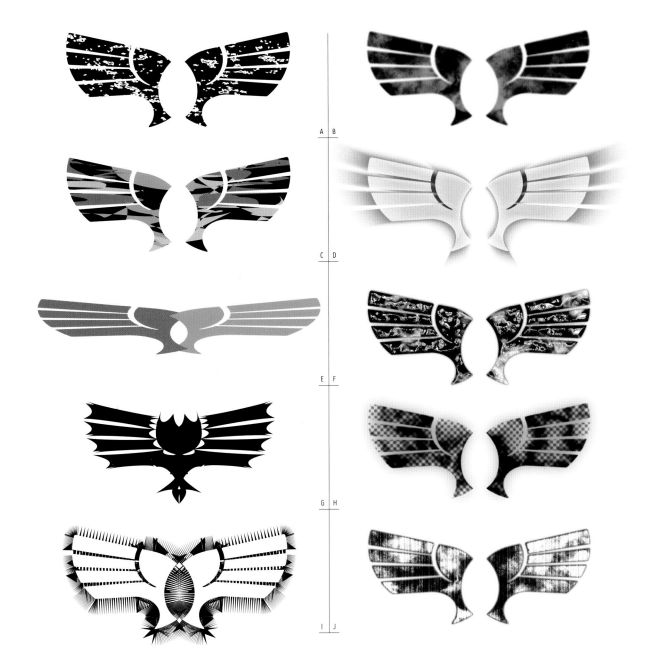

A B

C D

E F

G H

I J

Subtle dimension

The wing theme of the last two spreads concludes here with a series of dimension-conveying explorations. The effects demonstrated on the opposite page are understated—along the lines of what might be employed to subtly enhance a corporate logo or whenever low-key implications of depth are being sought.

One thing to keep in mind when applying any sort of visual effect to a symbol (dimensional or otherwise) is that stylistic treatments of this kind are subject to the whims of fad and fashion—just like the stylistic treatments that are applied to hair and clothing. What's the best way to keep tabs on trends in the world of logo design (whether the trends are related to stylistic treatments, color combinations or methods of illustration)? By paying attention. Take note of the logos that appear at the fore of mainstream media, make a point of regularly looking through periodicals and books that feature the work of leading designers and mentally chart the rise and fall of the styles, trends and fads you observe.

[A] The low-key dimensional conveyances of this symbol are derived from its subtle inner glow (applied in Illustrator and set to black) and a light gray drop shadow. [B] A colored highlight and a dark inner shadow have been applied to this design using Photoshop's Bevel and Emboss effects. [C] Bevel and Emboss effects were also used to add a look of depth to the components of this icon. The wing was shaded using Gradient Map controls. [D] How about layering translucent and colored copies of a design? [E] Illustrator's transformation controls were used to spin, skew and resize these wings to form a stacked arrangement. Drop shadows were added to bolster the dimensional look of the composition. [F] The glossy, protruding ellipse containing this icon was created using Photoshop's Bevel and Emboss effects along with shading from a Gradient Map adjustment layer. [G] A static repetition of overlapping icons, each colored using Illustrator's Gradient panel. [H] A small grey ellipse has been placed below this icon to lift it from the page. (It's interesting to note how much impact this ellipse has on the presentation of the wing above it—cover the ellipse with a finger and note how the icon suddenly appears stuck to the page's surface.)

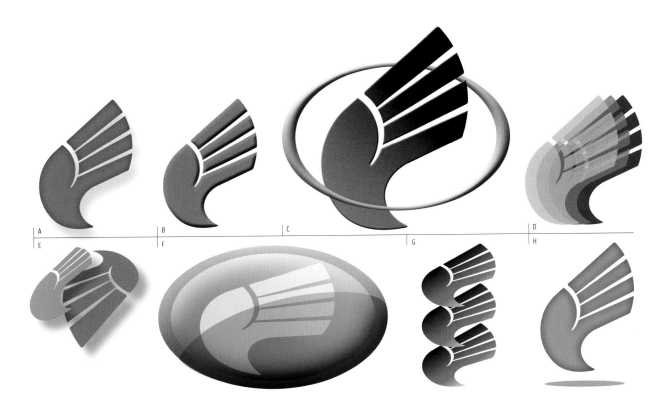

A

E

B

F

C

D

G

H

Drawing from photographs

Just because you're not an illustrator doesn't mean you can't illustrate. The trick is to work within the skills you possess and to use aids when necessary.

Say, for instance, you have a bicycle company as a client, and the owners of the company want an image of one of their classic cruisers as part of their logo. Here's an idea: Borrow one of the client's bicycles, photograph it from several attractive perspectives, choose your favorite shot, import it into a program like Illustrator or Photoshop and trace its form loosely or precisely—depending on the look you are after. (FYI: There's no need to feel guilty about taking a creative shortcut like this; card-carrying illustrators do it all the time.) Each of the illustrations at right was created by using the photo at the top of this column as a drawing template.

[A] An icon created by importing the photo at left into Illustrator and loosely re-creating its components with shapes drawn with the PEN tool. **[B]** Here, further options have been explored: The bicycle from the first sample has been placed inside a square and different colors have been applied to each of the design's negative spaces. **[C]** In this sample, the freely drawn bicycle from before has been recolored and placed beneath a precise linework rendering (created by closely following the contours of the photographed subject using Illustrator's PEN tool). **[D]** What about transplanting an illustrated subject into a custom-drawn environment? **[E]** A silhouetted bike stands between the sun and a cast shadow. The shadow was created by applying a light tint to a copy of the bicycle and then stretching and skewing the tinted silhouette into position as a shadow. Once the shadow was in place, its form was blurred using the Gaussian Blur effect. **[F]** Photoshop's Watercolor filter was used to create this faux-painted version of the scenic design featured in [D].

A

D

B

E

C

F

Alternate Endings

After you've invested time photographing a subject and carefully tracing its contours, take full advantage of the fact that you now have a ready-to-go vector drawing that can be finalized in all kinds of different ways: Don't even think about getting up from the computer until you've explored at least a half dozen of the billion or so possibilities that await discovery.

Changing course

Feeling stuck? Has your search for a logo solution lost momentum or become disoriented? If so, then here are two choices: hunker down and keep at it or change course (at least temporarily).

Tenaciously staying after a particular creative goal is often the best—and sometimes the only—way of coming up with a successful design. But what if an apparent lack of progress leads to feelings of frustration that threaten to have you clawing at your monitor or climbing the walls of your cubicle? What then? Well, what about taking a mind-clearing (and potentially problem-solving) detour down alternative creative avenues? For example, say you are feeling absolutely fed up with your (thus far) unfruitful search for a symbol-based design: How about changing course and redirecting your concepts and ideas to the development of a monogram or a type-heavy signature?

If your alternative explorations lead to an effective solution, great: problem solved. If not, then at least your search into fresh creative territory will have given you a break from whatever it was that was frustrating you before—a break that might well lead to break-*throughs* when you get back at it.

Want to look into a few alternative design approaches? Use these six designs (borrowed from other chapters of *The Logo Brainstorm Book*) to help spark ideas. Also, thumb through the rest of this book's content—there are plenty more ideas where these came from. **[A,B]** Getting nowhere with your search for a leaf-based symbol design? How about creating a leafy monogram instead? What is the subject matter of your current logo project? How might the subject look if it were interpreted as a stand-alone monogram, as a component within a decorative pattern or as an ornament inside a typographic construction (as seen in sample **[A]** on page 259)? **[C,D]** Ready for a complete change of course? Would the client be receptive to a purely—or mostly—typographic signature? **[E]** Is there a ready-made decorative element (such as this design's ornate archival enclosure) that could be used in place of a custom-crafted icon? **[F]** Instead of featuring your design's symbol as a stand-alone icon, how about employing it as a background element for a signature's typography?

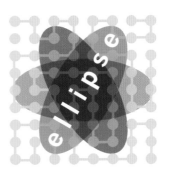

81

Perfection is achieved,
not when there is nothing more
to add, but when there is nothing
left to take away.

Antoine de Saint-Exupéry

Less is a bore.

Robert Venturi

So, which is right? Should you take away from your signature's design until it is pared down to its absolute compositional and thematic essentials or should you elaborate on its presentation until the thing teeters near the bursting point of visual anarchy and conceptual overload? That all depends on who is paying for the design, who the logo is being targeted at, and the kinds of visual messages the design ought to be conveying. A signature intended to represent a financial institution, for instance, should probably present itself in a more straightforward and to-the-point manner than, say, a logo for a street carnival or a brew pub. What is the right approach for the logo you're working on? Something simple, something complex or something in-between?

Paint, pigments and pixels

Are you skilled with paint and brushes? Comfortable using pencils, pens or pastels? Are you savvy with digital tools that mimic hands-on mediums (pressure-sensitive tablets and their associated drawing implements, for instance)? If you answered *yes* to any of the above—and if you believe that your client's audience will react positively to an artistically rendered icon—then how about creating it by hand? (If you answered *no* to the above questions and still want to incorporate a hand-rendered icon into your logo design, then consider hiring a freelance illustrator to finish the project.)

[A] A pressure-sensitive Wacom tablet was used to create this hand-crafted illustration: Several layers of translucent pixels were built up to achieve the painterly outcome shown here. **[B]** This illustration, like the first, was made using a Wacom tablet and Photoshop's virtual brushes. Photoshop controls were used to make the pixels behave very much like ink from a pen and watercolors from a brush. **[C]** A Wacom tablet was also used to produce this freely rendered design (one of Photoshop's pressure-sensitive, multi-width brushes was selected as the right tool for this job). When working digitally, an artist can try as many times as they like to come up with just the right brush strokes for an illustration like this—unsuccessful strokes can be eliminated with a click of the mouse. **[D]** Special photographic effects were applied in Photoshop to give this image an illustrative appearance and to layer it over a photo of weathered wooden planks. The design's trans-lucent circles were also added in Photoshop.

Are you one of those designers who doodles, draws and paints just for the fun of it? If so, keep it up—chances are, you've already discovered that these for-fun creative activities enhance your ability to produce money-making logos and illustrations.

If, on the other hand, you're a designer who rarely or never creates art outside of work, then how about putting a sketchbook in your purse, shoulder bag or back pocket and using it for doodles, sketches and thumb-nails whenever the mood and the opportunity strike? And what about picking up some watercolor supplies and doing still-life paintings and abstract compositions instead of watching television once in a while?

A tip for those readers who are new to hands-on media: Go easy on yourself! Quality counts when you're designing logos, but when it comes to this kind of loosely structured creative exploration, it's much more important to simply investigate, experience and enjoy.

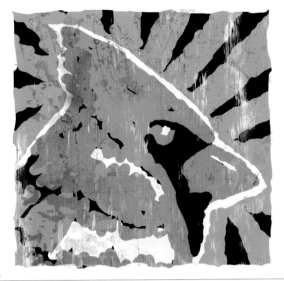

A | B
C | D

Suitable for framing

If you've decided on a hands-on, illustrative approach for an icon, consider creating the artwork—or having it created by someone else—at a size that will be suitable for framing. Your client may be delighted to hang the artwork in their office (if you decide not to hang it in your own, that is). Just make sure that the detail in the full-size artwork is bold and clear enough to hold up properly when it's reduced to a size suitable for letterheads, small advertisements and web mastheads.

The illustration on the opposite page was made by aligning the differently colored impressions of three different hand-carved linoleum blocks. Translucent inks were used so that additional colors would occur where the inks overlapped.

Digital slicing and dicing

How about using an old-time woodcut illustration as icon-building material? Archival illustrations are abundantly available in books, catalogs and online.

The opposite page features several samples that were created by scanning and digitally altering old-time images. Some of the illustrations were combined with other renderings (both archival and modern) in an effort to produce intriguing, silly and visually entertaining outcomes.

[A] An old-time architectural drawing, repeated, reflected and placed inside a subtle rectangular enclosure. **[B]** A nonsensical two-wheeled pushmi-pullyu (pronounced "push-me, pull-you"—the name of a mythical creature from the world of Dr. Dolittle). This fanciful bicycle was created by digitally cutting and mirroring parts of an archival illustration. **[C]** Ever hear of a jackalope? The legendary chimera of the prairie with the head and body of a rabbit and the horns of an antelope? What about creating a fabled creature of your own by cutting and pasting parts from two or more vintage animal renderings? **[D]** A thought bubble provides an intriguing link between two very unalike illustrations. **[E]** Styles are also mixed in this sample where a contemporary rendering of a coffee cup has been adorned with details from an archival map and framed with a pen-and-ink drawing of a wreath. **[F]** Then again, how about building an icon from like-minded illustrations? Here, the wreath from the previous design has been digitally paired with a similarly styled drawing.

Once an archival illustration has been scanned from its printed source, it can be digitally cut, colored, transformed and reinterpreted in Photoshop or Illustrator. The cupid figure at far left was scanned from a catalog of old-time images. Once the wing had been isolated using Photoshop's selection tools, it was exported to Illustrator where LIVE TRACE tools were used to artistically redraw its features. The resulting graphic is one that could be effectively used as a stand-alone symbol or as an element within a more complex icon design.

A

B

C

D

E

F

From photo to icon

Got a digital camera? Know how to use it? Why not employ photographic material of your own to create an icon? Images can be inserted into logos as-they-are or they could be digitally enhanced using Photoshop tools and treatments. Photography-based icons can be created from the content of a single image or from elements borrowed from several.

Anyone who takes a lot of photos would probably agree: The best photo opportunities are usually the ones that pop up in the most unlikely places and at the most unexpected times. For this reason and others, many designers consider it a must to keep a pocket digital camera on hand—in a purse, shoulder bag or pocket—just about wherever they go. That way they'll be able to capture images of potentially useful subject matter whenever and wherever it shows itself. Over time, these designers are able to build a tremendously useful cache of photos that can be used for inspiration and reference, as well as for ready-to-use images for layouts and logos.

[A] A strong graphic icon of a vintage automobile has been created by selecting and cutting its form from a photo, pasting the selection into a document of its own and treating it with Photoshop's Threshold effect. [B] Photoshop's Posterize effect was used to simplify and strengthen the colors of this cut-and-pasted automobile. The vehicle was tilted, horizontally flipped, treated with the Motion Blur filter and placed above a blurred elliptical shadow to animate its appearance. [C] The main subjects of two photos have been combined to create this reality-bending icon. Handy with Photoshop's selection tools and its special effects? If so, then there's no limit to the kinds of visual shenanigans you can pull off in pursuit of eye-catching imagery (provided, of course, that you work for clients who appreciate this sort of thing). [D] Two vignetted interpretations of one photograph: one tinted with a classic sepia tone, the other treated in a more colorful and contemporary manner using Photoshop effects. Take a good look at your options when applying digital effects to photos. Which ones produce the most appropriate visual and thematic results? [E] What about silhouetting a photo's subject matter and placing it atop a custom-made backdrop? [F] How about using Photoshop filters to convert a photo into a faux illustration suitable for presentation as something like a postage stamp or a postcard?

A

B

C

D

E

F

Halftoning

Halftoning is the process of converting the light-to-dark values of a continuous-tone image (such as a photograph) into a pattern of tiny dots. The light and dark areas you see in a halftoned image have been achieved by varying the size of its dots. All the images in this book—except for those printed using only solid black ink—are made from halftone dots. The black-and-white images have been built using dots of black ink. The color images have been composed from a mixture of cyan (blue), magenta, yellow and black dots.

Designs can be infused with themes of nostalgia and kitsch through digital effects that render images with enlarged halftone dots—a look that mimics the appearance of newsprint images from an era when the technology of the day required that halftone dots be printed at exaggerated sizes.

The four images on the opposite page demonstrate a range of effects that can be achieved through the options offered by Photoshop's Halftone Filter effects.

Above: A photo, prior to being treated in Photoshop.
Below: The halftone treatments that were used to create the variations at right.
[A] Filter>Sketch>Halftone Pattern>Circle
[B] Filter>Sketch>Halftone Pattern>Dot
[C] Filter>Sketch>Halftone Pattern>Line
[D] Filter>Pixelate>Color Halftone

A	B
C	D

Building with photographic elements

Here's a fun thing to try—either for the creation of an icon or just for the sake of artistic exploration. Start by using Photoshop tools to select an element-of-interest from one of your digital images. The element could be the main subject of a photo or just a detail (such as the ornate iron spike circled at right). Feather the edges of your selection slightly and then copy-and-paste it into a new document that offers plenty of extra white space. Next, see what sorts of designs you can create by rotating and repeating the element. Experiment with different rotation angles (if want your circular design to contain equally spaced copies of your element, divide 360 by the number of times you want the element repeated in order to find a specific angle of rotation), explore different points around which your element is spun and also experiment with different orientations for the element itself (horizontal, vertical, flipped, angled, etc.). Once you've created a few appealing outcomes, try applying Photoshop adjustments and effects to the designs to see how they might be improved and finalized.

[A] An ornate spike was selected from the above image, pasted into a new document, converted into a silhouette and then repeated and rotated to form this decorative design. **[B]** A more complex version of the previous icon was made by layering colored duplicates of the symbol and adding a white glow to the center of each copy. **[C]** Here, detail within the photographed spike has been strengthened using contrast controls. Copies of the object were then rotated and colored to produce this symbol. **[D]** A copy of the previous icon has been desaturated, rotated and moved to an underlying layer to produce this intricate and dimensional design. **[E]** How about aiming for an even more complex creation? Inner glows and outer shading were added to this multi-layered version of the symbol before its proportions were stretched with Photoshop's transformation tools. **[F,G]** Once a symbol has been created in Photoshop or Illustrator, consider exploring the distortion effects offered through these programs. The Twirl and Glass effects were used to fashion the outcomes shown here.

A

B

C

D

E

F

G

Mixing it up

Most of the icons in this chapter were created according to a single stylistic approach: simplified, dimensional, linework-based, modern, archival,
photographic and so on. A few of the chapter's samples were built around
a pair of contrasting styles for the sake of infusing the design with notes
of humor or intrigue. But what about going
a step further? How about combining three
or more different styles in order to come up
with an even more "out there" design? The
illustrative icons featured on this spread
were assembled using a contemporarily
rendered cartoon character, an archival
etching of a frame and an enhanced and
colored photograph of a cloud.

When offering a client a complex and colorful
logo solution such as the example at right, consider
accompanying the design with a simplified version
such as the one above. The simplified version might
come in handy for applications that cannot be eco-
nomically produced in full color.

Enclosures

Chapter 6, Emblems, pages 240–267, features many examples of both simple and complex enclosures. A few basic enclosures are presented here as well. Why here, in the midst of a chapter that's about designing symbols? It's because enclosure possibilities are well worth considering—even if it's only in the back of your mind—whenever you're working on an icon. Enclosures can be employed to add finishing touches of visual interest to a symbol, used to bolster an icon's thematic conveyances, put in place to generate notes of contrast and added to help stake out a symbol's territory within a complex signature.

The enclosures shown here are straightforward and only a few have a significant effect on the stylistic appearance and the thematic conveyances of the icon they accompany. For a look at enclosure treatments that are more detailed and thematically charged, investigate the samples presented in chapter 6.

[A] A solid shape wrapped with a thin line: a tried-and-true style of enclosure that's been around for a long, long time. **[B]** An icon built from circle-based shapes that echo the visual nature of its enclosing backdrop of rings. **[C]** An ornate platform of filigree contrasts nicely with the bold shapes of the bumblebee floating above it. **[D]** What about reversing your tightly rendered icon from something like a rough-edged textural backdrop? **[E]** The extra-bold linework around this icon creates a form-following enclosure. **[F]** How about using a photo as a backdrop? What shape should the photo be? Should it have crisp or vignetted edges? Should it be colored or black and white? **[G–K]** One icon, five basic black enclosures. Consider backdrops that harmoniously echo the shape of your icon, as well as those that provide contrast. **[L]** How about applying transparency effects to your icon's enclosure and placing it *above* the icon? **[M]** Keep in mind that an enclosure need not completely enclose its contents. **[N]** Copies of the waveforms featured in this monogram have also been used to create its loosely jointed border. **[O–Q]** Linework: explore your options: thick, thin, dark, light, colored, black, gray, single, double, triple, one weight or multi-weight. (See page 55 for a large selection of linework-related ideas.)

A

B

C

D

E

F

G

H

I

J

K

L

M

N

O

P

Q

A committee is an animal

with four back legs.

John le Carré

If you had to identify, in one word,

the reason why the human race

has not achieved, and never will

achieve, its full potential, that word

would be *meetings*.

Dave Barry

P resenting an idea to a committee—and then dealing with the group's feedback—is kind of like serving a volleyball with a bag over your head: You aim the ball in what you believe is the right direction and (if the ball has landed in bounds) you then stand and wait, wondering from which direction it will return and if it will be gently tapped into your arms or if it will be spiked into your gut. "Surviving Your Next Committee Meeting" is not a class that's usually offered in design schools, but it is a subject worth learning about if you want to get ahead in the business of commercial art. Learn by observing designers and account executives who have a reputation for positive and productive communication skills: Watch them at work and take note of how they gracefully handle challenging group dynamics while building consensus.

Heads

It's doubtful that any subject of artistic expression has been explored half as thoroughly as that of the human form. And even though people and their parts have been exhaustively rendered for centuries using everything from the pigment of berries to pencils, paints and pixels, there remains an infinite number of new and expressive ways to convey the appearance of humans.

This spread—and the three that follow—are designed to initiate brainstorming forays into the infinite realm of symbols that portray or suggest humans, human features, human emotions and human experiences.

Use the ideas shown on the opposite page to help brainstorm for ways of depicting human heads—along with the many sensations and emotions that are commonly and distinctly expressed through facial expressions.

[A–C] The head of an ancient greek statue enclosed in an ornament-topped circle and treated to a modernizing series of Photoshop effects. [D] What about searching archival sources for a beautifully rendered human face or feature? This Renaissance-era da Vinci portrait has been framed with an ornamental design from the nineteenth century. [E] Interestingly, faces can be drawn without including the subject's eyes, ears, mouth, nose or skin. [F] A pair of interacting twins built from a 1950s illustration. The symbol's backdrop adds a sense of energy to the design while compositionally connecting the two faces. [G] Skulls make faces, too, and if dressed appropriately, they can appear as something other than menacing. [H] Photoshop's Threshold and Solid Color treatments have been used to convert a photograph of a costume-wearing human into this gargoyle-esque caricature. [I–M] Explore the endless human (and human-like) representations that can be built from basic shapes. [N] The senses of hearing, sight, smell and touch can all be represented through abstract and representational symbols. [O] A cut-paper style of illustration achieved by loosely tracing a photograph with straight segments from Illustrator's PEN tool. [P] Fright, as expressed through a comic book style of rendering (a style that can be used to take the edge off of what might otherwise be an image's disquieting content). [Q] How about making a nod to earlier times with an illustrative approach borrowed from a previous decade? [R] Multilayered linework and patterns of dots define the form of this tattooed character. [S] Illustrated flames have been merged with a high-contrast portrait to lend connotations of expressive energy to this design.

A B C D
E F G H
I J K L M
N O
P Q R S

103

Hands

Hands are incredibly versatile—both as extensions of arms and as subject matter for icons. Renderings of hands are often used to represent organizations involved in people-centered concerns such as healthcare, social services and community relations. Depictions of hands can be used to express notions as varied as connection, conflict, cooperation and rebellion.

Could a graphic rendering of hands be developed into your client's icon? If so, what might the hands be doing? How should they be rendered? One hand? Two hands? A pattern or a design made from many hands?

[A–C] What about filling the form of a hand with a pictorial or decorative image? [D] An elliptical icon built from the translucent forms of graphically rendered hands. [E] A stylized set of hands arranged in a revolving gesture that generates suggestions of continuity, flow and connection. [F] Overlapping spirals serve as the outwardly expressive palms of this overlapping pair of hands. [G,H] What could be placed in the palm of your hand-based symbol? Brainstorm the endless options. [I] Here's a long-shot idea that just might suit a project you're working on: What about developing a creature-like icon based on a human feature? [J–L] Many icon possibilities exist within the realm of utilitarian-style renderings of hands. See anything here that sparks a useful idea? [M] How about adding a raised-and-clenched fist holding a FILL-IN-THE-BLANK to your inspirational (or kitschy) logo design?

Ever sketch a hand? How about using one of your hands to make a drawing of the other? What about doing this every day for a month? The sketches could be quickly rendered or they could be carried out in an exacting and detailed manner—whatever you have the time and energy for. The drawings need not be perfect or even good: The point of this exercise is not to produce exquisite renderings, but rather to improve your powers of observation and to sharpen the connections between your eye, your drawing hand and your art tools. And why not? Improved brain/hand/tool connections are never wasted on a graphic designer or a fine artist.

If you find this sort of exercise pleasurable, you might really enjoy drawing humans as a whole: Check into local figure-drawing classes or workshops (often available through community colleges, universities and artists' groups).

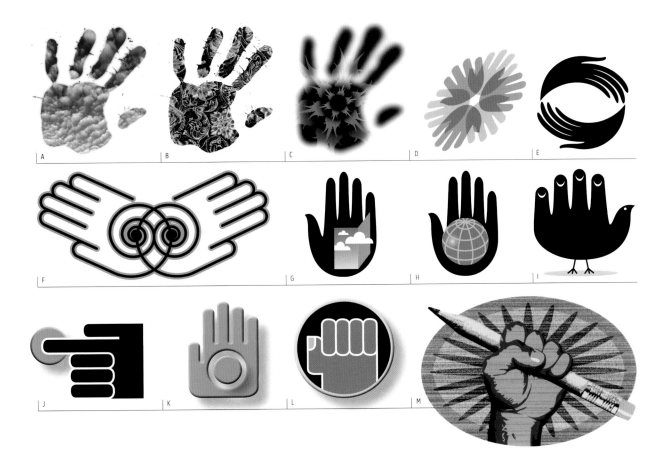

A

B

C

D

E

F

G

H

I

J

K

L

M

Eyes

Eyes make masterfully versatile subject matter for icons: Eyes are the conveyors of a vast range of emotions (love, fear, anger, compassion, indifference, zeal and so on); eyes are incredibly beautiful both in terms of their form and their function; eyes are standard equipment on a surprisingly diverse range of beasts, birds and bugs; eyes can seduce, smite, scintillate, swoon, startle and sway. The superlative eye: Have you considered using one or more as visual material for the icon you're working on?

[A] Hands as eyelids? Why not? **[B]** A curved shadow on the page itself defines the opening for this dimensional eye. **[C]** How about using a mask to hide the face behind a pair of eyes? **[D]** Consider highly abstract and geometric approaches when rendering any human component. **[E]** Would a non-human eye work best for your project? **[F]** A close up of a human eye, treated with Photoshop's Half-tone Pattern filter. **[G]** A decorative fan from one archival etching has been pasted over a woman's face taken from another. The fan adds visual and thematic interest while directing attention to the woman's eyes. **[H]** A minimally rendered eye peeks from behind the stylized foliage of a trio of leaves. **[I]** A glassy eye peers from inside the fiery fingers of a blackened sun. **[J]** Eyes and glasses as one—a continuous-line drawing created using a Wacom tablet and a digital brush.

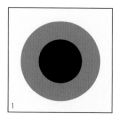 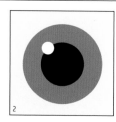   

There are many ways of illustrating eyeballs. Here's a sequence of images that show how different levels of complexity might be considered when creating a graphic rendering of an eye. **[1]** A circle within a circle may be all that's needed to produce a symbolic depiction of an eye. **[2]** The addition of a white highlight can by used to convey the reflective qualities of an eyeball. **[3]** A note of dimensional realism can be introduced by shading the outer perimeter of the iris. **[4]** What about heightening the realism of the eyeball by adding a subtle outer glow to a more detailed rendering of its highlight? **[5]** Additional shading and the inclusion of detail within the iris can enhance connotations of depth and accuracy.

A | B
C | D
E | F
G | H
I | J

The human figure

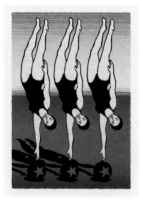

Have you ever found yourself in a dimly lit room and been spooked by a silhouette that appeared to be a human figure, only to find out that it was something like a coat hanging from a rack or an oddly shaped indoor plant? Why are people so visually sensitive to forms that look like they might belong to another human? It probably has to do with our instincts for both survival and connection: instincts that keep our senses on high alert for anything that suggests that another person may be near.

What this means to designers who are working on a human-oriented rendering is that they may be gifted with relaxed expectations of accuracy. And while creative freedom is always a good thing, it's rarely granted without a warning label of some sort. The cautionary advice here is this: Be mindful of the general proportions of the human body, even when you are rendering it in a highly stylized or abstract way. Aim for some semblance of accuracy unless your goal is to intentionally portray the body as something other than proportionately typical. Pay attention to conveyances of personality, gender, age and attire, as well, since these attributes are bound to be noticed and scrutinized by viewers.

Creating designs from figures

What about taking your human-based design and repeating it around a common point to come up with a decorative circular icon? The symbol may or may not appear as a collection of human forms at first glance, but, if rendered adequately, it should offer the true nature of its content as a pleasant surprise to viewers who spend more than a moment looking at it.

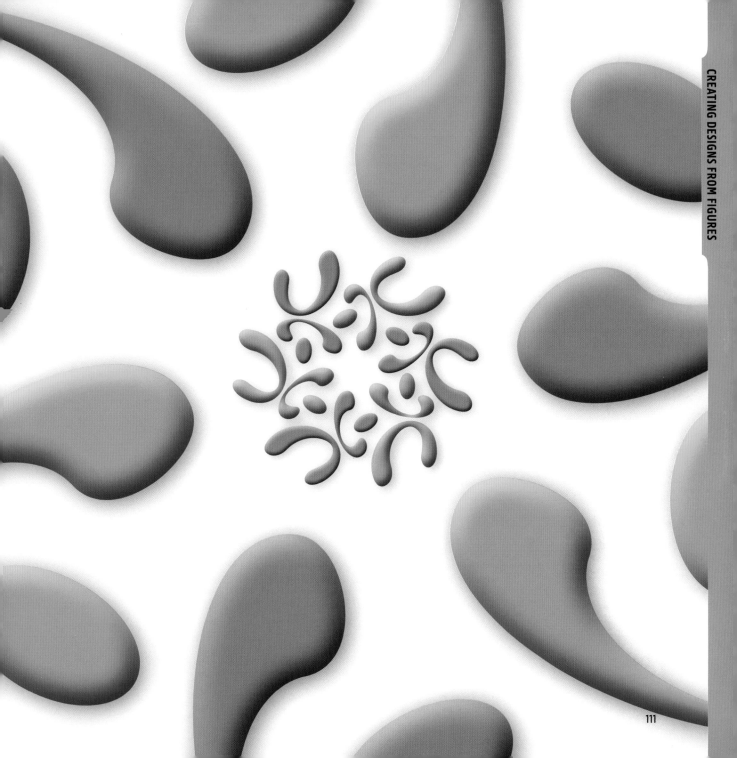

Exercises

Use the samples throughout The Logo Brainstorm Book *to help generate ideas as you seek solutions for these exercises. Make an effort to push your ideas into fresh creative territory—from thumbnail to finish.*

If you are interested in adding color to any of the designs you create for these exercises, consider checking out chapter 7, Color, pages 268–296, for tips and ideas.

REINVENTING THE CIRCLE

Page 35 features seventeen variations of a square. Your assignment here is to come up with seventeen variations of a circle (along with the circle's dimensional relative, the sphere).

- Each of your designs should deliver unique visual and thematic conveyances through its style and its means of rendering.

- You may add visual elements within or around the circle or sphere—as long as the additions do not obscure the circular or spherical nature of the design.

- Strive for as wide a range of conveyances as possible: Aim for connotations such as minimalism, complexity, elegance, crudeness, antiquity, industry and technology.

PATHFINDER ABSTRACTIONS

This exercise makes use of Adobe Illustrator's PATHFINDER operations, and if you are familiar with the PATHFINDER panel, it will provide you with a good opportunity to strengthen your skills with its set of controls. If you are new to PATHFINDER operations, spend a few minutes reading about them through Illustrator's Help menu and then jump right in: Hands-on experience is an especially good way of learning about this amazing and extremely useful set of controls.

- Begin by creating a few basic shapes in Illustrator: rectangles, triangles, polygons, circles and ellipses.

- Open the PATHFINDER panel and apply its effects to various combinations of shapes (use copies of the shapes so that you'll always have an original to come back to if needed).

- Combinations between identical and different shapes should be explored.

- Shapes may be resized or reproportioned as you work.

- Apply PATHFINDER operations to groups of shapes and also to the outcomes of other PATHFINDER operations.

- Free-flowing creative exploration is the goal here, and as you work, gradually seek from your many creations two or three abstract designs that fit into each of the following categories: bold and solid, light and airy, ornate and symmetrical, jumbled and asymmetrical.

PATHFINDER REPRESENTATIONS

Your client has asked for one stylized icon of an African animal and one of a native plant for use in their annual report. Illustrator's PATHFINDER panel should provide you with just the tools needed to produce this pair of icons.

- Choose one African animal and one native plant or tree.

- Use the Web and reference books to research the visual characteristics of your chosen subjects.

- Spend time getting ideas flowing with thumbnail sketches. This is where the real creative work begins, and—if done conscientiously and thoroughly—it will streamline the computer tasks that lie ahead.

- As you sketch ideas, aim for graphically simplified depictions of your subjects (use the samples throughout this chapter to help brainstorm for illustrative approaches).

- Feel free to focus on portions and details of your subjects (as opposed to rendering their entire forms).

- When you are ready, open Illustrator and its PATHFINDER panel and begin creating your icons.

- As with the previous exercise, start with an assortment of basic shapes as building components.

- As an option—if you are competent with 3-D soft-ware—think about also creating one or two of this exercise's subjects using a program of that type.

EXPLORING LINEWORK

This one is simple.

- Begin by creating a basic stick figure with 1 pt lines.

- Your stick figure may be standing, sitting or engaged in an activity.

- See how the look of the figure can be affected by altering the ways in which its lines have been rendered

113

(use the linework samples on pages 54–55 as starting points for your own stylistic explorations).

- Push your ideas to extremes, aim for quantity at first and then gradually narrow your designs down to your favorite half-dozen.

- Arrange your chosen set of figures in a row or in a stack and print them on a fresh document for presentation.

THREE'S A CROWD PLEASER

A client would like to see two versions of an icon that includes three stylishly rendered depictions of inter-acting humans. The client has asked that the symbol express energetic connotations of connection, that its figures appear as neither male nor female and that no strong indications of race are apparent in its beings. Other pictorial elements are welcome in the design, as long as the human figures are the icon's strongest features. Some suggestions:

- Begin your search for promising creative directions by coming up with a list of things your icon's figures could be doing, as well as a list of visual elements that could be incorporated into the designs.

- Make many thumbnail sketches before deciding which ideas are most deserving of further exploration on the computer.

- Investigate ways of constructing the icon's figures that involve PATHFINDER operations applied to basic shapes.

- Have a go at creating expressive characters using free-form drawing tools such as Illustrator's PEN tool.

- Consider using non-computer media such as ink or paint to create at least one of your designs.

- Aim for a variety: How about creating one of your ideas in an extremely simplified manner, and the other as a relatively complex assemblage of lines or shapes? What about stretching the rules and rendering one of your icons using only details of humans—hands, perhaps?

- Think about creating one of the icons by repeating the same figure three times to form an attractive inter-locking design.

- Investigate designs that are built from figures that are each doing something different.

- Pay special attention to the overall shape created by your trio of figures. Should the group fit within a circle or a square?

- Give thought to enclosures. Could one of your designs be placed within a decorative border or on top of a shape that's been filled with a pattern, an illustration or a photograph?

MIXING MEDIA

Got a digital camera? Know how to use Photoshop's selection tools and its Layers panel? If so, this exercise will allow you to employ your skills to fabricate an interesting and eye-catching icon from an ordinary object.

- Begin by taking a picture of a chair—a living room chair, a school chair, an office chair, any chair. (A simple backdrop behind your chair will make the next step easier.)

- Bring your image into Photoshop, select the chair, feather its edges slightly and cut-and-paste it into a new document above a white background.

- Before deselecting the chair, use the Select pull-down menu and choose "Save Selection." This will give you quick access to the chair's form later on.

- Next, have fun: Spend time pasting patterns, illustrations, solid colors, symbols and photos inside the chair's boundaries; use transformation tools to resize, reproportion and reshape the chair; consider using special effects to transform the look of the chair; try out a few different backdrops behind—and enclosures around—the chair's form; ponder the possibilities of a multi-chair icon.

- Come up with a half-dozen designs that look like icon-worthy material.

- Remember the lessons you learn here so that you can apply them when crafting photo-based icons and artwork in the future.

3 Monograms

CHAPTER CONTENTS

3   Monograms

A MONOGRAM is a letter or a set of initials used to represent a company, an organization or an individual. Letters from an existing typeface can be modified to create a monogram. Unmodified characters can be used as well—perhaps with their forms enclosed by linework, backed by a colored shape or surrounded with ornamentation. Monograms can also be created from scratch according to a project's stylistic and conceptual goals.

A company's initial(s) can contribute to a convenient logo solution since there is an inherent association between a monogram and the entity it represents. Be aware, however, that it would be a mistake to assume that creating a design from a

company's initial(s) is a sure-fire route to an outstanding logo. To be excellent, a monogram must adhere to the same criteria for success that applies to an abstract or a pictorial icon: It must attractively deliver appropriate thematic connotations while inciting the interest of its target audience.

The purpose of this chapter is to provide brainstorming material that will help you design effective monograms that are capable of meeting this criteria for greatness. For more about the crucial early-project work of evaluating a client's needs, assessing the preferences of their target audience and coming up with appropriate visual and thematic content, see chapter 1, Beginnings, pages 4–27.

In most cases, monograms are designed to appear along with a company's name in the form of a cohesive signature. Monograms can be placed above, below or alongside a logo's type or they can be made to integrate directly with its letters. Chapter 5, Type + Symbol, pages 196–239 and chapter 6, Emblems, pages 240–267 feature many different ways of combining monograms with typography—take a look at these chapters when you are brainstorming for ways of building a logo from a monogram (or an icon) and type.

Ready-to-go beginnings

Monograms can be built using letters taken directly from an existing typeface. Stock characters can also be modified in order to become monograms. If you are thinking about creating a monogram using a character from an existing typeface—whether or not the character is to be modified—your options are many and they are growing by the day: Digital media and the Internet have made possible a mind-boggling expansion of the number and variety of readily available typefaces.

So, where to begin? Where to launch your search for the perfect character to use as-is—or as a starting place—for a monogram? Begin by looking on your hard drive. Take a look at your fonts, one by one, apply anything that looks like it might have potential to both uppercase and lowercase versions of your client's initial(s) and save the most promising outcomes for further consideration. This will be a quick process if your are familiar with all the

fonts on your computer. If you are not well acquainted with your typefaces, this task may take some time, but it will be time well spent since it will improve your awareness of typefaces and their conveyances.

The Internet is the place to go if you want to look at fonts beyond what your hard drive has to offer. If it's your first time exploring the Web for fonts, be prepared to face a nearly overwhelming array of options—and also know that you'll probably be able to narrow the seemingly endless choices down to a useful few in an hour or two. Use search tools, as well as advice from other designers, to make your online font-searching experience as efficient as possible.

Interested in creating a monogram from scratch—a monogram that does not begin with a character from an existing typeface? Pages 127–139 feature many examples of custom-built monograms.

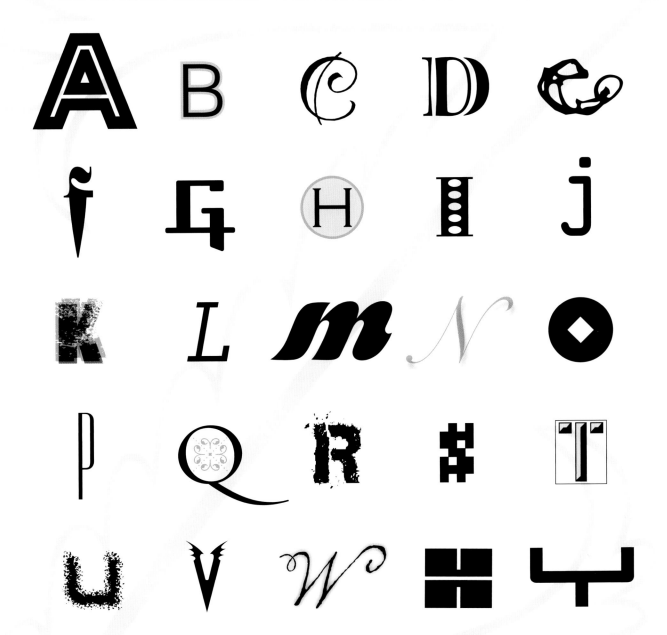

Letterform add-ons

It's amazing what something like an added swoosh, curl or ornament can do to the aesthetics and the thematic conveyances of a standard letterform. Monograms can be created by substituting part of a letter with a decorative or pictorial element, by elongating a character's stroke, by capping a detail with an expressive flourish, by continuing a serif or crossbar into a letter-enclosing border or by integrating a character with a pattern, an ornament or an illustration.

Letterform enhancements that connect harmoniously with the look of a character can be employed to boost the conveyances of a character's visual personality. Enhancements that contrast with the look of a character can also be sought—especially when seeking connotations of modernity, humor or tension. Choose decisively between treatments that promote feelings of unity vs. those that establish discordant associations: The lukewarm middle-ground between these two approaches tends to produce an impression of uncertainty.

[A] A spiraling extension has been added to this sans serif character. The capital *R* is a letter that's particularly well suited for the addition of embellishments. **[B]** Decorative enhancements need not touch letterforms. Here, an ornament integrates nicely with an *M* by virtue of its placement and proximity. **[C]** The tail of this *Q* has been replaced by a decoratively rendered leaf. Take a look at the letterform you are converting into a monogram. Could any of the character's components be replaced with pictorial material? **[D]** Instead of melding a stylized add-on with the form of a letter, how about laying it over top? **[E–I]** What about integrating a waveform, line, swirl or ornament into the structure of a character? The capital *A*, *N*, *M*, *G*, *E*, *F*, and *W* are ideal candidates for typographic restyling of this kind. **[J]** Contrast is the objective here: A showy and fine-lined typographic ornament has been bonded to an extremely bold sans serif capital. Conveyances of modernity and counter-culture can be delivered through mergers of contrasting styles. **[K]** A serif of this lowercase *m* has been extended to form a curly cornered enclosure. **[L]** How about producing a monogram by garnishing a letter with a few ready-to-go typographic dingbats? **[M]** Does the name of your client's business include a numeral? If so, what about stretching the definition of a monogram and creating one from its digit(s)? The bold and weathered *5* in this sample contrasts nicely with the classically styled typographic elements on which it sits.

Building letters from basic shapes

In chapter 2, Symbols, basic shapes were used to build abstract and representational icons. On this spread, shapes have been used to produce custom-crafted monograms. Any letter or number can be depicted through arrangements of basic geometric forms. Letterform-conveying designs of a more complex nature can be sculpted from basic shapes using Illustrator's PATHFINDER operations (see page 42 for more about these controls).

All of the finished designs on the opposite page were built from basic shapes, and while some were created using PATHFINDER operations and some were not, each was born and incubated on the pages of a sketch pad. Consider spending time brainstorming design directions through word lists and thumbnail sketches before moving ahead with any design project: Time spent with pen and paper at the beginning of a project almost always streamlines the computer-based work that follows. (See chapter 1, Beginnings, pages 4–27, for more about brainstorming with word lists and thumbnails.)

[A] A capital *C* that's been created by subtracting a circle from a square. [B] A rectangle and several diamonds were used to create this bold and toothy *E* (a character that could also be seen as an *M* or a *W*—depending on its orientation).[C,D] Instead of building a letter from basic shapes, how about creating a pattern of shapes and highlighting a character from within the arrangement? [E] What about reversing a letter from one or more basic shapes? The perfect half-circle curve of this monogram's *D* connects harmoniously with the circles from which it is reversed. [F] Bold lines and circular bends create the form of this tightly cropped character. [G,H] A modernistic *P* and *X* built from ellipses. On their own, monograms like these may or may not be seen as letterforms, but when viewed in conjunction with the name of the company they represent (as monograms usually do), their dual function as both letter and icon becomes evident. [I] A lowercase character neatly centered within a circle. The monogram's visual personality has been enlivened by coloring its negative spaces. [J] Directional arrowheads have added implications of vitality and movement to this lowercase design.

A	B	C	D	E
F	G	H	I	J

Dimensional incarnations

Here, a selection of depth-invoking treatments has been applied to the two-dimensional monograms from the previous spread.

Dimensional effects, like color combinations and font styles, are continually coming and going from the fore of fashion. Keep tabs on what seem to be the most popular and effective ways of conveying illusions of depth. Is it through a certain kind of drop shadow? Stacks of translucent elements? Bevel or emboss treatments? Op-art illusions (such as the Escher-like twist of the S in [F]). What about perspective-mimicking special effects like Photoshop's Spherize treatment? Shelf life is important for a logo: When creating a signature, avoid choosing typefaces, colors or a special effects that are likely to grow prematurely stale in the eyes of its audience.

[A] How about stacking translucent copies of your monogram to create a dimensional feel? Illustrator's transparency controls were used to set the blend mode between these shapes to "Multiply"—a setting that mimics the look of layered panes of translucent plastic. [B] Subtle connotations of depth are delivered through this design's use of graduated tints and transparency effects. [C] Photoshop's Spherize treatment was applied to the dot-pattern design from the previous page to create the protruding monogram shown here. [D] InDesign's Bevel and Emboss effect was applied to this pattern's letter-forming triangles to set them apart from the monogram's non-dimensional tiles. [E] The only thing that sets this design apart from its white backdrop is a subtle drop shadow. [F] A character that has been rendered in a perspective-conveying op-art style. [G] Inferences of connection and an understated sense of dimension are lent to this monogram by allowing one of its free-form shapes to pass through the hole in the other. [H] The orb at the center of this monogram has been given a simple 3-D makeover by shading it using Illustrator's Gradient controls. Additional implications of depth have been conveyed by varying the widths of the elliptical paths that encircle the orb. [I] Would a few illustrative touches improve the visual impact of your monogram? Something to indicate a glossy dimensional surface and reflected light? [J] As if made from a standing ribbon of plastic or metal, this lowercase *d* pops from the page by virtue of its dimensional shading and a cast shadow.

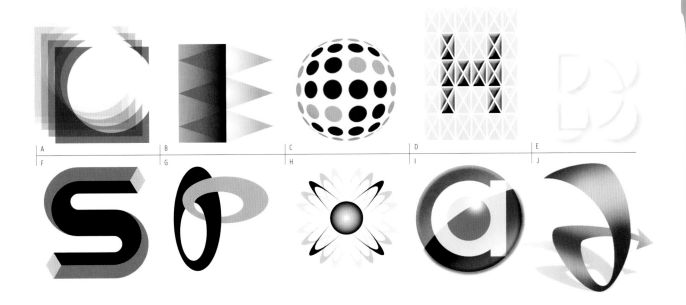

A | B | C | D | E
F | G | H | I | J

Pushing it further

The previous page featured custom-made letterforms created from basic shapes. On this spread, the creative parameters are widened to include characters made from free-form shapes, arcs, swirls, ornaments, photographic material and watercolors.

Interested in coming up with a monogram that pushes the norms of character design? Use the examples on this spread to initiate avenues of investigation that extend into whatever far-flung regions of creative experimentation you wish to explore.

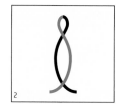
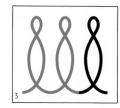

Letterform creation need not always be a complex and time-consuming task: The *W* featured at the top of the opposite page was built in just three quickly executed steps. **[1]** A curving line was created from portions of two ellipses. Care was taken to make sure the top and bottom terminals of the line were perfectly vertical (an important detail for the upcoming steps). **[2]** A copy of the curving line was horizontally flipped and joined to the original. The vertical terminals at the tops of the two lines allowed them to be joined seamlessly (a visible joint would have occurred if the terminals had been angled). **[3]** Two copies of the new shape were made and the three identical shapes were joined at their bottoms to finalize the monogram.

[A] All it took to create this ornate capital was a couple of spirals. The spirals were repeated, flipped, mirrored and joined with linework. A thick, contour-following enclosure was added to complete the design. **[B]** As shown at left, this letter was also created using a bare minimum of visual components. The monogram could be flipped vertically to be seen as the letter *M*, rotated clockwise to read as an *E* or turned counter-clockwise to become the number *3*.**[C]** A capital created using decorations borrowed from a font of typographic ornaments. **[D]** A thorny creation built from four different elliptical arcs. The monogram's structure is revealed by the dark blur radiating from its form. **[E]** How about photographing real-life objects that have been arranged to look like a letter? **[F]** A character constructed from a flowing mix of waves and curls. Each component of this monogram was built by either applying PATHFINDER operations to solid ellipses or by combining segments taken from line-drawn ellipses. **[G]** And now for something completely different: What about pulling out your watercolors and brushes and rendering a portrait of your client's initial(s)? How about using oil paints, pencils or pastels instead? What about sculpting a letter from paper, clay or junk? **[H]** A complex weave of interacting ellipses forms this cord-like circular monogram. **[I]** This dot pattern first appeared on page 37 as an icon design. It reappears here as a reminder that icons can often be seen as both abstract symbols and as monograms.

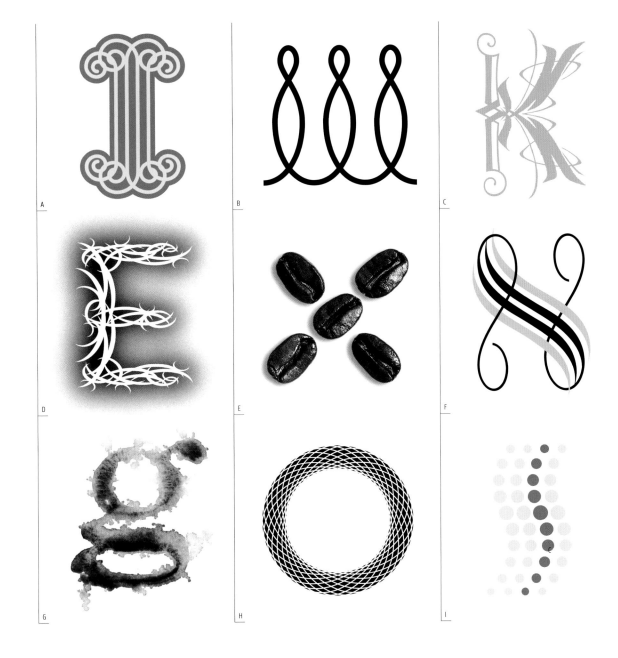

A

B

C

D

E

F

G

H

I

Pictorial typographic creations

How about coming up with a monogram that simultaneously portrays the client's initial(s), conveys aspects of what the company does and delivers positive connotations about the business? A well-designed pictorially based letterform can do all this and more.

An excellent way to begin work on an illustrative monogram is by making a list of nouns, verbs and adjectives that are in any way connected to what the client does and how they do it. The lists should cover what the company produces, what services they provide, anything they use to get their work done, how they interact with their clients and, if applicable, interesting details about their work environment, office building and mascot. (See pages 17–19 for more about coming up with idea-launching lists for logo projects.) Once you've thoroughly brainstormed these topics, use your word lists to provide material for thumbnail sketches that will lead to aesthetically pleasing and thematically targeted pictorial monograms.

[A] Several of the custom-crafted monograms on the previous page were created using multiple copies of just one or two components. Same goes for this ornate design: A single leaf, a circular berry and a few curls of filigree have been repeated, rotated and repositioned to form the decorative assemblage seen here. **[B]** Is it an *h*? Is it a chair? Yes—and yes. Is there an object related to what your client produces or does that could be rendered to appear as their initial(s)? **[C]** What about creating an icon from illustrated components? What type of product does your client produce? What tools do they use? Is the company named after a creature or a thing? Make a list of potential subject matter and consider creating a monogram using renderings of one or more of the items you come up with. **[D]** A company name has been placed with this monogram to emphasize a point: In many cases, it's permissible to create a monogram that may or may not instantly read as a letter—as long as the design also functions as an intriguing and appropriate icon. For example, viewers of this logo's jumping-figure icon may not realize that it could also be interpreted as the letter *Y* until they notice the name of the company it represents.

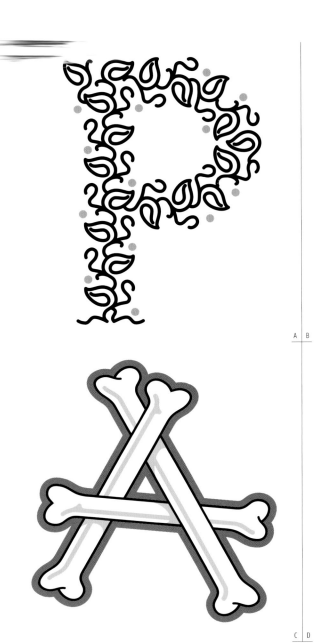

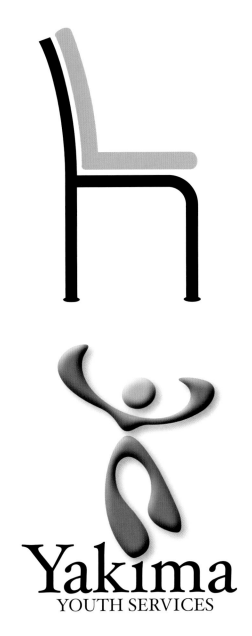

A | B

C | D

133

Filling letterforms with images

Stripes, patterns, illustrations, symbols or photographs: What about filling a letterform with an interesting visual and calling it a monogram?

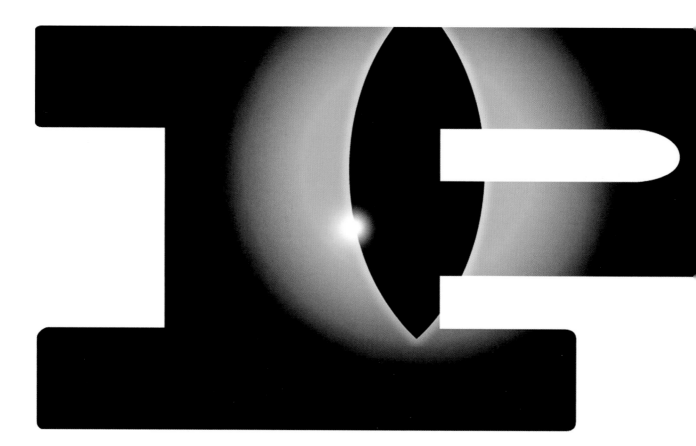

The only real valuable thing is intuition.

Albert Einstein

This thing of intuition—it's your friend when you feel that what you are working on isn't correct. And then that same tool can tell you how to make it correct. And that same tool will tell you when it is correct.

And there's no other way to get there.

David Lynch

Intuition is the product of things you know you know, things you don't know you know, everything you knowingly or unknowingly feel, plus a whole bunch of unnamed things that you'll probably never know anything about (unless, that is, you somehow find a way to cleanse those grimy doors of perception William Blake wrote about a couple centuries ago). Sound complicated? It's not: Creative intuition simply *is*, and it will continue to exist whether we pay attention to it or not. But pay attention we must if we—as designers—hope to produce logos, posters, websites, advertisements and packaging that will not only produce commercially desirable results but will also add to the earth something others will enjoy looking at and contemplating.

Whatever works

So how about it? What are a few other out-of-the-ordinary design directions you could explore as you brainstorm for ways of creating an effective and eye-catching monogram? This spread continues the theme of the previous page by offering a few more outside-the-box ideas—presentations that make a point of not fitting into commonplace stylistic categories. (And none of this is to suggest that there's anything wrong with looking for solutions that *do* fit within relatively normal design parameters; these spreads are simply offered as reminders that outlier approaches are equally worth considering.)

[A] Hand-drawn circles contrasting with a precise rectangle form this modernistic capital *Q*. [B] What about reversing an initial from an unusual backdrop to create a distinctive monogram? [C] A script *S* rendered from scratch using Illustrator's PEN tool. How about developing a free-form rendition of your client's initial(s)? [D] Is there a way of conveying an important aspect of your client's business through a pattern of abstract symbols? Connotations of connectivity and action are lent to this character through its randomized internal pattern of linked circles. [E] A visually-active letter created by layering numerous and variously colored copies of a single free-form shape. The translucency of the shapes lends a feeling of depth to the design. [F] A monogram made using the same 3-D document that was employed to create the futuristic icon on page 53. The document's forms were relit, recolored and repositioned to produce this typographic design.

Adobe Illustrator offers a variety of blend modes through its Transparency panel's pull-down menu (blend modes are settings that affect how an element interacts with whatever is below it). Color Burn was chosen from the panel's pull-down menu to determine how the colors of the layered shapes in [E] mix with each other. Other blend modes could have been chosen for this design, and the samples below show a comparison between the Color Burn mode and four others. Investigate your options whenever you employ blend modes.

COLOR BURN

HARD LIGHT

DIFFERENCE

SCREEN

MULTIPLY

Pictorial additions

How about using a symbol, ornament or illustration to boost the visual and thematic appeal of the monogram you're designing? Pictorial elements can be inserted into, cut from, added to or placed behind typographic characters.

When considering what kind of visual to add to a letterform, explore different approaches: The addition could be a photograph, an illustration or a graphic symbol; the addition could be representational or abstract, silly or serious, precisely rendered or casually drawn; the addition could stylistically complement the letterform or it could contrast with it.

Also, investigate a variety of compositional relationships between your letter and its pictorial component. Which should dominate the design—should it be the letter or the image? Be decisive in this matter so that your typographic and pictorial elements will not fight with each other for viewers' attention.

[A,B] Eye-catching monograms can be made by filling the interior spaces of letters with images, patterns or photos. **[C]** A monogram made from ready-to-use components: a typographic ornament and a script capital. **[D]** With a few minor modifications and the addition of a elliptical halo, this ampersand has been converted into a monogram that delivers lighthearted conveyances of both good and evil (see page 205 for an example of how a typographic character like this might be incorporated into a corporate signature). **[E]** Instead of placing images or symbols into a letter's negative spaces, how about sculpting the spaces into shapes that represent something related to your client's business? **[F]** The needle and thread used in this monogram were first featured on page 61 as a stand-alone icon. The needle has been integrated into the form of this lowercase *f* by acting as its crossbar. When working on icons, be open to whatever monogram-producing opportunities arise. **[G]** An *e* crowned with an ornament taken from a symbol-based font. Many designers keep several such font families on their hard drive where they can be accessed for all kinds of instant visual material. **[H]** Sometimes, all it takes is a subtle modification to one component of a letter to turn it into an expressive monogram. **[I]** What about devising an intriguing interaction between a typographic character and illustrated components? **[J]** A pictorial element has replaced part of the crossbar of this lowercase *t* to turn it into an organically inclined monogram. When working on symbols, save unused designs in a folder on your computer—they just might come in handy for a future monogram project.

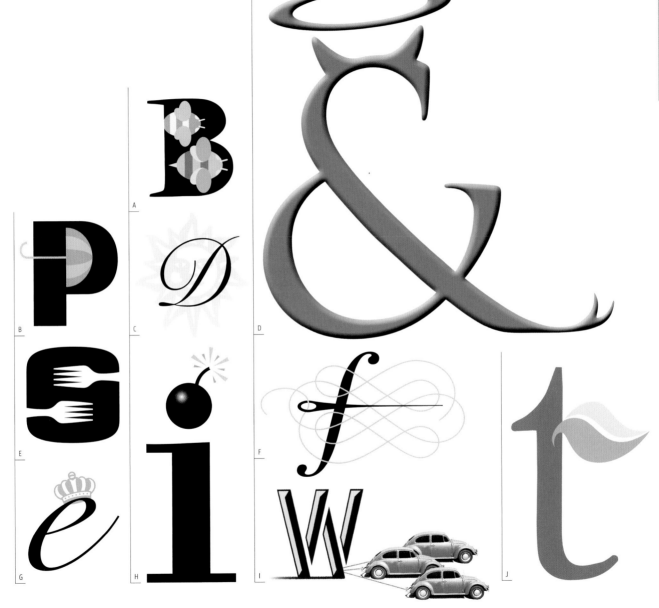

Extroverted enclosures

How about placing a letter inside a flamboyant enclosure to create a monogram bursting with extroverted energy? The decorative swirls of this monogram's enclosure are responsible for nearly all of its visual and thematic conveyances (remove the enclosure and all that would remain would be a standard *W* from an ordinary serif font). Interested in surrounding your typographic character with an attention-grabbing ornamental, illustrative or photographic enclosure? If so, use the samples on this spread and the next—as well as those featured throughout chapter 6, Emblems, pages 240–267—to help brainstorm for ideas.

Enclosure ideas

Enclosures can be employed to quietly support the thematic conveyances of typographic characters. Enclosures can also be allowed to dominate a monogram's design while delivering their own connotations of style and persona. The monograms on this spread tend toward the latter sort, and all feature unmodified characters borrowed from existing fonts. Would a visually expressive enclosure be an effective carrier of the conveyances you are trying to bring to the monogram you're working on?

 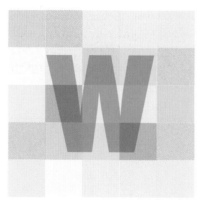 

Which should stand out most strongly in your enclosed-monogram design, its letter or its enclosure? How much difference should there be between the visual strength of each? Take the time to investigate a variety of answers to compositionally significant questions like these before deciding which approaches produce the most appealing outcomes.

Pairing letters harmoniously

Visual associations between letters can be established by allowing their forms to touch or overlap, by connecting them with ligatures or flourishes, by fitting them together in the form of tightly structured compositional units, by enclosing them within unifying shapes (shapes that could be filled with photos, decorative designs or solid colors) and through the use of connecting symbols such as ampersands, plus signs and arrows.

This spread and the next provide a look at letter-linking strategies that could be applied to multiletter monograms (FYI: the dictionary definition of a monogram doesn't limit these graphic entities to just one character). Consider these stylistic and structural approaches—along with those that have been applied to this chapter's single-letter monograms—when brainstorming ways of creating a design from more than one character.

[A–C] How about completing the form of one letter with an extension from another? **[D]** An aesthetically pleasing union of two characters. Take a good look for whatever letter-linking opportunities might exist between the characters of the monogram you're working on. **[E]** Letters can be stacked as a means of joining them. Transparency effects help ensure the readability of these overlapping characters. **[F]** A stylized butterfly created by adding antennae to a pair of capitals (one of which that's been horizontally flipped). **[G]** What about cropping letters inside simple geometric shapes? Seek aesthetically pleasing croppings that preserve the characters' legibility. **[H]** The same typographic ornament that crowns a letter at the bottom of page 141 has been employed here as a theme-setting visual connector between two characters. **[I]** A vertically arranged monogram presented in the style of a mathematical fraction. **[J]** A circular line forms a simple enclosure around this pair of neatly overlapping capitals. (Interested in exploring other enclosure options? See chapter 6, Emblems, pages 240–267.) **[K]** Consider pairing characters of different weights to form a monogram. The *x* in this design has been underlined as a means of providing emphasis and to add a touch of variety to the letters' presentation. **[L–O]** Working for a client that has the word *and* in their name? Explore your options as you look for ways of making a monogram from their initials.

A reminder: Use the samples on this spread—as well as those featured throughout all of *The Logo Brainstorm Book*—as mere starting points for your own creative explorations. Look at a sample and think, *How can I apply this idea to the project I'm working on: How can I stretch this idea, morph this concept and reshape this approach until it turns into a solution that's purely my own?*

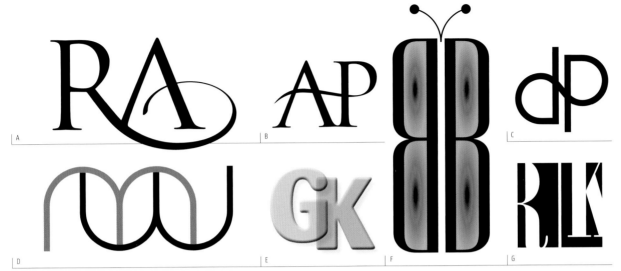

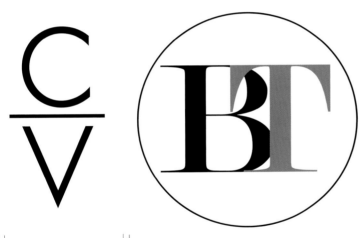

A

B

C

D

E

F

G

H

I

J

K

L

M

N

O

Pairing contrasting letterforms

Most of the samples on the previous page feature visually harmonious pairs of letters from a single typeface. On this spread, not-like characters have joined to create monograms that convey notes of diversity. Some of these pairings retain a feeling of harmony in spite of the differences between their letterforms. Other combinations assume an ambiance of visual and thematic intrigue through intentionally discordant associations.

Are you working for a client whose business emotes a divergent mix of qualities? How about designing their logo as a monogram that includes typefaces capable of expressing different aspects of their corporate personality? For instance, what about combining a bold serif character with a delicate script initial to convey both brawn and beauty? What about pairing a letter from a creatively rendered contemporary font with a classic serif capital to represent a forward-thinking company with a proud reputation for sound business practices?

[A] Some letters can be flipped in order to become other letters. This monogram's lower character has been distorted so that it appears as a watery reflection of the upper letter. Are you lucky enough to be working on a monogram that includes a mirror-image set of letters? If so, look for unique visual and thematic opportunities. **[B]** A pair of custom-crafted initials that produces visually pleasing conveyances of both opposition and harmony: Contrast is generated through the differences between the lower character's bold right-angle construction and the upper letter's linework-based rendering; a feeling of like-mindedness arises from the similar proportions and the straight-edged construction of the two characters. **[C]** Contrast is embraced in this design as an ornate script capital is allowed to interrupt the form of an extremely bold serif character. **[D]** The sense of visual opposition emanating from this monogram is era-based: A classically rendered *O* from a previous century encloses the digitally derived form of a lowercase *b*. **[E]** This strongly contrasting pair of characters has one thing in common: the thin diagonal line from which they both emerge—a line that both joins and separates them.

A

B

C

D

E

Exercises

Use the samples throughout The Logo Brainstorm Book *to help generate ideas as you seek solutions for these exercises. Make an effort to push your ideas into fresh creative territory—from thumbnail to finish.*

If you are interested in adding color to any of the designs you create for these exercises, consider checking out chapter 7, Color, pages 268–296, for tips and ideas.

SIMPLE BEGINNINGS

The Gimmet Corporation is a contemporary-minded company that operates a half-dozen Five-star hotels, a chain of cutting-edge clothing stores and a limousine service. They are asking you to develop three stand-alone monograms using the letter *G*. The monograms should visually connect as a family and each should represent one of the corporation's three businesses.

- The monograms could be created from scratch or they could be built using characters from one or more typefaces.

- Consider adding ornate or pictorial extensions to your characters, enclosing them within a shape or a decoration or filling them with an abstract or representational visual.

BUILDING WITH SHAPES

This exercise is meant as an excuse to enjoy some creative playtime using letterforms. Your assignment is to develop a set of monograms featuring any five letters of the alphabet. Not only is this exercise a good way to practice monogram development, it's also a nice introduction to the sophisticated art of typeface design.

- Construct your characters using geometric shapes: rectangles, triangles, polygons, ellipses, etc.

- PATHFINDER operations from Illustrator or InDesign may be employed to convert the shapes from geometric to free-form.

- Digital effects may be applied.

- Aim for visual and thematic connections between the monograms—as if the characters were to be used for a single expressive font.

GOING DIMENSIONAL

Familiar with 3-D software? If so, as an optional extension of the two previous exercises, rethink and redesign one or two of the monograms from those projects as eye-catching dimensional forms.

Interested in taking one of your designs even further? How about utilizing your 3-D software's capability of producing animated sequences? What about creating a short video using one of your monograms—an animation of the kind that's often used to present a company's logo at the end of television commercial or video?

BUILDING A PRESENTATION

Your job here is to create a monogram for a seaside amusement park using the letter *A*. The letter may be presented as a capital or a lowercase character. The client has asked for designs that reflect the festive atmosphere of the park through depictions of carnival rides, seaside activities and abstract symbols that generate conveyances of fun and excitement. They have also requested that your presentation include:

- a total of three designs for consideration
- one design that is made—entirely or in part—using non-digital media such as paint, ink or cut paper (scan or photograph your non-digital art to bring it into the computer for finalization)
- one design of extreme horizontal or vertical proportions that incorporates hints of confetti or fireworks
- one design that features an expressive enclosure as its dominant visual component

Look through this chapter's samples to help generate ideas. Begin your creative process by making lists of potential subject matter and thumbnail sketches (see pages 17–19 and 22–24 for more about early-project brainstorming practices).

ADDING IMAGES

A company called Filigree wants to see their *F* developed into a monogram. And, since the company's specialty is indoor plants, their logo committee has asked that a leaf (or leaves) be incorporated into the monogram. The committee disagrees, however, on the following:

- whether the *F* should be a capital or lowercase letter
- whether the featured leaf (or leaves) should be from a weeping fig, a dieffenbachia or a ficus
- whether the leaf (or leaves) should be a photograph, a tight illustration or a stylized icon

Your task is to create three monograms for presentation— ideas that address each of the variations mentioned above.

PAIR AND GROUPS

Ready for a set of creative calisthenics? Create monograms from the following pairs and sets of characters:

- *G* and *H*,
- *q* and *j*
- *A*, *B* and *C*

Anything goes with these designs: Use whatever fonts you like and consider applying digital effects and color to your monograms.

- Strive for fresh, creative territory with each of the designs you create.
- Aim for notably different thematic and visual conveyances from each monogram.

- Use the multiletter designs on pages 146–147 to help generate ideas.

A MONOGRAM OF YOUR OWN

You are the client for this exercise: Create a personal monogram using your first, last and—if desired—middle initial(s).

- Develop and produce a monogram that represents characteristics of your day-to-day personality or one that affirms positive aspects of your professional persona.
- Spend ample time brainstorming for content ideas and stylistic approaches. Begin by making a list of possible visuals that could be incorporated into the design, as well as a list of thematic conveyances your monogram should generate.
- Fill a page—or several—with thumbnail sketches and don't move on to the computer until you have at least three ideas that you're feeling especially excited about.
- The initials could come from a typeface or they could be created from scratch; the design could be simple or complex; the letterforms could be accompanied by abstract, decorative or pictorial elements; the charac-

ters could be linked, stacked, interlocked or presented apart from one another.

- Your goal is to come up with a monogram that has significant potential for real-world applications such as personal or professional stationery or as part of a blog's masthead.

COLLECTING INSPIRATION

This exercise has a beginning but no end, and it is guaranteed to improve your powers of observation while simultaneously providing you with a valuable visual resource of inspirational and educational visuals. Here's how it works:

- Start by making a point of carrying a pocket digital camera with you as often as possible (a good-quality cellphone camera will also work).

- Take pictures of intriguing letterforms wherever you find them: printed in advertisements and books, contained within logos and emblems, scrawled as graffiti or rendered by hand.

- Save and categorize your images using photo organization software such as iPhoto or Aperture.

- Consult your collection of inspiring letterforms when you are working on monograms.

Also, be sure to snap photos of anything you come across that happens to look like a letter—things like an antique doorhandle that resembles an ornate *P* or a chair's cast shadow that looks like a lowercase *h*. You may be able to use these photos as ready-to-go material for monograms, custom-made drop caps (the oversized characters that sometimes appear at the beginning of paragraphs) or other typography-based design projects.

4 Typographic Logos

CHAPTER CONTENTS

4 Typographic Logos

A SIGNATURE'S TYPEFACE gives voice and personality to the design. This is especially true in the case of a logo that's purely or mostly typographic—whether the signature's letters come from a ready-to-go font, they are customized versions of existing characters or they have been created from scratch.

Have you been assigned to develop a type-only logo? If so, then it's important to understand that the word *only* need not be seen as a downgrade or a restriction. Purely typographic logos are more than capable of declaring themselves in attractive and memorable ways without the help of icons or images: The well-designed letters of beautifully assembled words are perfectly able to convey

an incredibly diverse span of thematic messages through aesthetics that range from exquisitely gorgeous to intentionally coarse. In fact, it's safe to say that if there's a particular emotion, sentiment or expression you are trying to deliver through a type-only logo—and you haven't yet found a font that delivers the conveyances you're looking for—then you simply haven't spent enough time looking.

Many different styles of typographic (and mostly typographic) logos are displayed on the pages that follow. Use the samples ahead to help generate ideas as you brainstorm for ways of creating aesthetically pleasing and thematically targeted type-only logos, and also when you are considering

different ways of presenting the typography in designs that include pictorial material.

Five company names have been used for all of this chapter's signatures. The clear differences in the presentation of each of these company names from one spread to the next should serve as a reminder of the countless ways in which the typographic logo you are working on could be developed.

Existing typefaces

Here, the five company names being used for this chapter's typographic explorations have been set using existing typefaces, and each of the samples could be considered ready-to-go signatures. Is it a good idea to use an existing typeface—without alterations, embellishments or additions of any kind—for a client's logo? Sometimes it is and sometimes it's not. If a straight-from-the-shelf typeface perfectly fits the needs of a logo you're working on, then it just might be the ideal choice.

A downside to this strategy is its potential lack of uniqueness, since other companies may have chosen—or will choose—the same font for their logo. In the end, trust your design sense and your business savvy to tell you if an existing typeface could be an appropriate choice for your all-type or your type-plus-icon design.

Looking for ways of altering typefaces or creating custom letters for a purely (or mostly) typographic logo? The rest of this chapter provides plenty of brainstorming material along these lines.

Alley Cat
Debonair
Nucleus
Whirl, Twirl & Spin
Biotic

AlleyCat

ALLEY CAT

ALLEY CAT

Debonair

Debonair

Debonair

nucleus

Nucleus

NUCLEUS

whirl, twirl, & spin

whirl+twirl+spin

WHIRL TWIRL & SPIN

Biotic

Biotic

BIOTIC

Simple modifications

The typefaces from the previous page are re-presented on this spread with backdrops, outlines, enclosures, underlines, special effects, pictorial elements and altered letters. Treatments like these can be used to transform stock characters into unique—and possibly more expressive—letterforms.

The modifications and additions shown here are relatively simple, but they may be just the sort of things needed to put the finishing touches on a logo you are working on. Take a look at each of the samples on the opposite page and translate the essence of what's being shown into specifics that could be applied to your project. And, as always when using this book, don't hesitate to let your ideas wander into whatever creative territory best suits the evolving vision of what you want your design to become.

[A] How about completing your type-only logo with a simple enclosure? The enclosure could be designed to contain all, most or some of the signature's letters. **[B]** The visual impact of this logo's light and free-form characters has been bulked up by wrapping the letters with a thick form-following fill. **[C]** Illustrator's Outer Glow effect was used to add a soft blush of color around the perimeter of this design. **[D]** What about incorporating a decorative underline as a finishing touch? **[E]** The geometric austerity of this logo's letters contrasts nicely with the design's playfully colored accordion-style backdrop. **[F]** An ornately rendered backdrop amplifies the elegant and artful conveyances of the gracefully crafted typeface used here. **[G]** How about applying a digital treatment to your typographic design? Illustrator's Distort filters were used to optically bulge this signature. **[H]** Subtle angular alterations were made to many of this font's vertical strokes to give its letters a more distinctive appearance. **[I]** Illustrator's Gradient panel (with its pull-down menu set to "Radial") was used to shade the interior of this signature's type. **[J]** Would a dimensional lift improve the appearance of your typographic logo? **[K,L]** Photoshop's transparency controls and Motion Blur filter were used to visually emphasize the literal meaning of these logos' words. **[M–O]** Why be a stickler for strict definitions? Why not consider adding subtle symbolic or pictorial elements to your "type only" design?

A

B

C

D

E

F

G

H

I

J

K

L

M

N

O

Family considerations

Got a font that you're considering as a finalist for a typographic logo? Great. Now, before blazing ahead with your creation, be sure you are using the most thematically, aesthetically and proportionally appropriate version of the typeface. Many fonts come in more than one style and in a variety of weights. Which style and weight would work best for your design? Should a condensed or expanded version of the typeface be used? What about employing more than one version of the font within a design? Does the typeface offer alternatives for certain letters, and would any of these substitute characters improve the appearance of the signature? Are you using a font that includes symbols, illustrations or ornaments? Could any of this visual material be added to your design's typography?

Also, be sure to consider options in terms of how your logo's letters are presented. Try out different amounts of kerning and leading and give thought to widening or narrowing the proportions of your font's characters—a little or a lot—using software controls .

[A] Bold characters, tightly kerned. **[B]** A line of lowercase italic letters with regular kerning. **[C]** Lowercase characters and a letter-replacing ornament. (The typeface used here is Bodoni Antique Regular and the flower is from a collection of Bodoni typographic ornaments.) **[D]** Capitals set with extremely tight kerning. **[E]** Lowercase characters positioned with exceptionally wide kerning. **[F]** A heavy font displayed in uppercase and lowercase with normal kerning. Note how the light shading of the letters reduces the visual impact of the characters' bold forms. **[G]** A set of bold capitals that has been stretched horizontally (or squashed vertically—depending on how you look at it). Typographic purists might consider it blasphemous to alter the proportions of characters as beautifully designed as these heavy Bodoni specimens, but then again, designers have always been a rule-breaking bunch, so why not consider it? **[H]** A playful hint of personality has been added to this line of highly condensed capitals by inserting a lowercase *i* within their ranks—and dotting the *i* with an expressive asterisk. **[I]** How about creating a type-only logo using letters taken from various members of an extended font family? What about assembling letters from several typefaces?

Debonair

debonair

deb❀nair

DEBONAIR

d e b o n a i r

Debonair

DEBONAIR

DEBONA*R

debonAir

Customizing letters

People are drawn to things that stand out from the crowd through attractive and unique qualities. Why not cash in on this naturally occurring favoritism by daring to be different? How about customizing some or all of your font's characters? What about creating your signature's letters from scratch?

Use this spread—and the several that follow—to help brainstorm for character-customizing treatments and letter-creating techniques that could be applied to your logo's typographic elements.

[A] Here's one way of turning a type-only logo into something more unique: convert one of its characters into a symbol. **[B]** What about filling a design's letterforms with a pattern, a symbol, an illustration or a photo? **[C]** The characters in this logo are 100 percent custom. Are you comfortable creating the individual letters of your client's name? If so, go for it. If not, how about hiring help? **[D]** A stencil font has been created by removing portions of some letters and cutting gaps in others (a step-by-step description of the process used here is shown below). **[E]** A character in this type-only design has been modified to convey the essence of the logo's meaning. Note how a color change—rather than a space— has been used to delineate the logo's words.

Illustrator's PATHFINDER operations are useful for making alterations to letterforms and for preparing them for upcoming modifications. The stencil-like characters in **[D]** were created by applying PATHFINDER operations to stock letterforms. **[1]** The letters were initially set in Futura Light. **[2]** A pair of rectangles were created to prepare for the upcoming PATHFINDER treatments. **[3]** The two rectangles were positioned over the letters prior to subtracting their forms from the characters' shapes. **[4]** "Minus" was chosen from the PATHFINDER panel to complete the modifications.

A

B

C

D

E

Embellishment

Decorative and pictorial embellishments can be used to amplify or redirect a word's visual and thematic expressions. The elegant persona of a word rendered in a traditional serif font, for example, could be amplified by adding gracefully swirling extensions to one or more of its characters; the word's conveyances could also be countered by somehow connecting its characters with matter-of-fact geometric linework.

What kinds of embellishments could be added to your design? Swirls, swashes, lines, decorations, ornaments, symbols, patterns or pictures? Should the additions sprout from letterforms or should they sit over, under or alongside the characters? How should the type and the add-ons interact? Harmoniously or with connotations of contrast?

[A] A fine-lined extension from this logo's first letter melds seamlessly with an extension coming from its final character. Modifications were made to both letters to accommodate their elegant double-line add-ons. **[B]** Ornate swirls originate from within this logo's line of words while decoratively framing its characters. **[C]** The shaded forms of gracefully rendered decorations contrast nicely with this logo's ultra bold characters. The decorative swirls used here were taken from Illustrator's Symbols panel and the designs were colored using the program's Gradient controls. **[D]** The simple letterforms that were custom-crafted for the "nucleus" logo on the previous page were modified to produce the more complex design seen here: Once you've taken the time to create letters for a logo, be sure to also spend time exploring different ways of finalizing and presenting them.

It's hard to beat the grace of an ellipse, which is exactly why you should consider using them as guides when adding decorative swirls to letters. Begin by developing a reasonably tight sketch of the design you want to create and then scan the sketch and import it into a vector-based program like Illustrator. Add ellipses over the top of the scanned image—on a layer of their own—wherever they might be used to establish the look of a loop or a curve (the blue ellipses in this sample indicate where placeholder ellipses were positioned prior to creating the logo's final sets of swirls). Once the ellipses are in place, cut them where necessary, add connecting segments and fine-tune the look of the custom-crafted swirls until you are fully satisfied with their grace and flow.

DEBONAIR

A

whirl, twirl and spin

B

biotic

C

nucleus

D

169

Waiting for inspiration is for amateurs.

The rest of us just show up for work.

Chuck Close

Eighty percent of success is showing up.

Woody Allen

The secret to getting ahead is getting started.

Mark Twain

The ultimate inspiration is the deadline.

Nolan Bushnell

There you have it: job advice and occupational observations from four creative individuals known for the breadth and the quality of their work. Quoted here is an astonishingly prolific modern artist; a movie man who has written, directed and acted in over 150 films; one of the most beloved and oft-quoted authors to have ever lived and an innovator/engineer who played an essential role in bringing computers into the everyday lives of humans. Pretty straightforward counsel, wouldn't you say? But then again, maybe that's the point—that the foundation of a job well done is a combination of showing up for work, diving into the project at hand and completing it according to deadline. After all, without these components of a day on the job, how would brilliance ever show itself?

Pictorial add-ons

The definition of a type-only logo is stretched beyond the breaking point on this spread where simple pictorial and symbolic additions have been added to straightforward typography. Why include designs that feature images and symbols in a chapter primarily devoted to typographic logos? It's to shake up the book's flow in the same way you should be willing to shake up and rethink any logo project whenever a creative impulse suggests—and then proves—that a change of course may lead to a better solution.

Are you working on a type-only design? What would happen if an icon or an ornament were added in a way that amplified the visual personality of the design's typography? Is it a notion that's worthy of a few minutes of consideration or are you feeling confident that your present creative course is best?

[A,B] Working toward an all-type logo solution? What about exploring the possibility of adding a subtle image or an icon to the design? Who knows, you just might stumble upon an idea that's too good to pass up. **[C]** Have a *C*, an *O* or a *Q* in the group of letters you're working with? How about filling the interior of one of these characters with an image or a symbol? (More ideas like this are featured on pages 222–223.) **[D]** Could your typographic logo be reversed from a silhouetted illustration? Should certain letters of the logo be used as part of the image? **[E]** A twirling top acts as an expressive dot atop each lowercase *i* in this design. Make a mental habit of giving at least a moment's consideration to altering the dot of any lowercase *i* that appears within a logo you're working on. **[F]** A typographic ornament has been converted into a tree-top extension for this design's uppercase *T*. **[G]** A sense of contrast is injected into this design by completing the form of its roughly rendered lowercase *t* with a precisely drawn trio of leaves. **[H,I]** Orbiting ellipses and a group of atom-like orbs conceptually connect with the meaning of the word used in these two designs. Does the logo you are working on include words whose meaning could be hinted at through imagery?

DEBONAIR

A

B

AlleyCat

C

D

E

BIOTIC

F

biotic

G

NUCLEUS

H

nucleus

I

Word as image

What about pursuing a solution that is equal parts image and type? How about presenting a meaningful aspect of your client's business through a rendering that also happens to read as the name of their company or organization? Brainstorm the possibilities through word lists and thumbnail sketches.

Hand-drawn lettering

What if you were to custom-render all—or part—of your client's logo using either traditional tools (pen, brush or pencil) or by digital means? How about mixing media and creating the signature's letters with hands-on tools and then finalizing the characters in Photoshop or Illustrator? Regardless of how you choose to create your logo's characters, explore styles of rendering that are casual, calligraphic, ornate, minimalist, precise, geometric, free-form, neat and messy.

[A] How about grabbing a felt pen or another kind of writing instrument and hand-rendering your logo—lettering, icon and all? **[B]** Ellipses were used to dictate the forms of this design's symbol and those of its custom-created letters. **[C,D]** Illustrator's versatile PEN tool was used to create the characters used in both of these designs. The PEN tool is an amazingly adaptable creative instrument: If you are not already familiar with this tool, it may be well worth your while to spend time learning about its functions and capabilities. **[E]** All the characters in this logo were created by hand: The first letter was made with pen and paper and the remaining characters were built using Illustrator's shape-creation tools.

Few designers have the skill to simply sit down with pen in hand and render a ready-to-go piece of handwriting or calligraphy. Are you working on a project that calls for a piece of hand-lettered text? Have doubts about your skill as a hand-letterer? Try the following routine. Set a large pad of paper in front of you and write your word(s), dozens of times, at approximately the same size. Once you have a large selection of attempts to choose from, look through your work and place a mark next to the best renderings of each letter (or sets of letters). **[1]** Next, take a knife or a pair of scissors, cut out your most promising characters and set them aside. **[2]** Tape or glue your selected letters into words. **[3]** Scan your creation and use Photoshop tools to finalize the composition, to adjust the spacing between letters, to remove shadows from the image and to adjust the overall contrast of the design.

A

B

C

D

E

177

Informalization

Just because there are numerous fonts whose every character exhibits heavenly ideals of perfection, and just because there are quite a few typefaces that are an almost etherial mix of geometric precision and aesthetic grace, it doesn't mean that you—a mortal graphic designer working on a logo for a start-up company that may or may not be around for the next five years—are required to choose one of these divinely inspired typefaces for every signature you create. Neither does it mean that you are banned from tampering with the look of immaculately conceived letterforms with mischievous add-ons, fills or structural modifications. It's the modern era and logo creation has evolved ("devolved," some might say) into a state where pretty much anything goes—as long as the resulting design is appropriately worshipped by its target audience.

[A,B] Two type-only logos, both rendered using off-the-shelf typefaces that imitate the look of spontaneously drawn letterforms. For the sake of believability, alterations were made to the letter *i* in both logos. Why? It's because the logos are meant to look as though they were rendered off-the-cuff, and the appearance of two identical letters within the designs could convey hints of inauthenticity. **[C]** What about filling the negative spaces of a casually rendered typeface with colors? How about filling the spaces with patterns, illustrations or photos? **[D]** Expressive swirls and swooshes lighten the mood of the heavy and solid sans serif capitals used here. **[E]** Speaking bubbles communicate on many levels: They communicate through words, through font styles and through visual treatments that have been applied to their words and to the speaking bubbles themselves. **[F]** The characters in this logo began as hard-edged geometric letterforms. Photoshop's distortion effects and its Difference Clouds and Blur filters were used to roughen the letters' edges and to give them an inky watercolor appearance.

A BIOTIC

B biotic

C DEBONAIR

D WHIRL&TWIRL&SPIN

E nucleus

F ALLEYCAT

179

Letters and shapes

When considering ideas for a logo's typography, turn your thoughts—at least momentarily—to the topic of shapes. Is there a way of constructing the letters of your client's name using basic geometric forms or simple free-form designs? What about inserting the characters into a set of either identical or unalike shapes? How about enclosing the entire signature inside a shape that either complements or contrasts with the look of its type?

[A] A blocky construction of geometrically inclined characters. A nice thing about creating your own letterforms is that you can freely make adjustments and additions while working in order to produce a compositionally cohesive and thematically expressive design. **[B]** Instead of building letters from basic shapes, how about using simple geometric forms as containers for stock characters? **[C]** Finely drawn ellipses and lines form this signature's characters. Once created, the letters were tightly packed to create a unified compositional element. **[D]** A small measure of this design's readability has been sacrificed in the interest of establishing a stylish and unique visual persona.

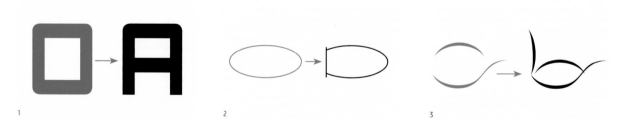

1

2

3

Typeface creation can be made less daunting if one or more specific shapes are allowed to dictate the structure and the style of a signature's custom-made characters. **[1]** Each of the letters in **[A]** is based on the form of a rectangle with sharp interior features and rounded external corners. **[2]** Horizontal ellipses have been cut, reproportioned and—in the case of the letter *O*—used without modification for most of the letters in **[C]**. **[3]** An elliptical arch and a free-form shape provide the basis for the characters in **[D]**.

A

B

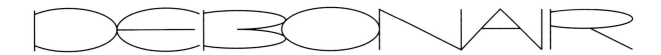

C

D

181

Adding dimension

There are all kinds of ways to lift letters, symbols and images from the surface of a page: Drop shadows, special effects, op-art styles of illustration and layering treatments can all do the trick. Looking for ways of adding a feeling of depth to the logo you are working on? Use the samples on this spread to help brainstorm for ideas, and keep in mind that the effects and treatments given to these custom-made characters could also be applied to letters from an existing typeface.

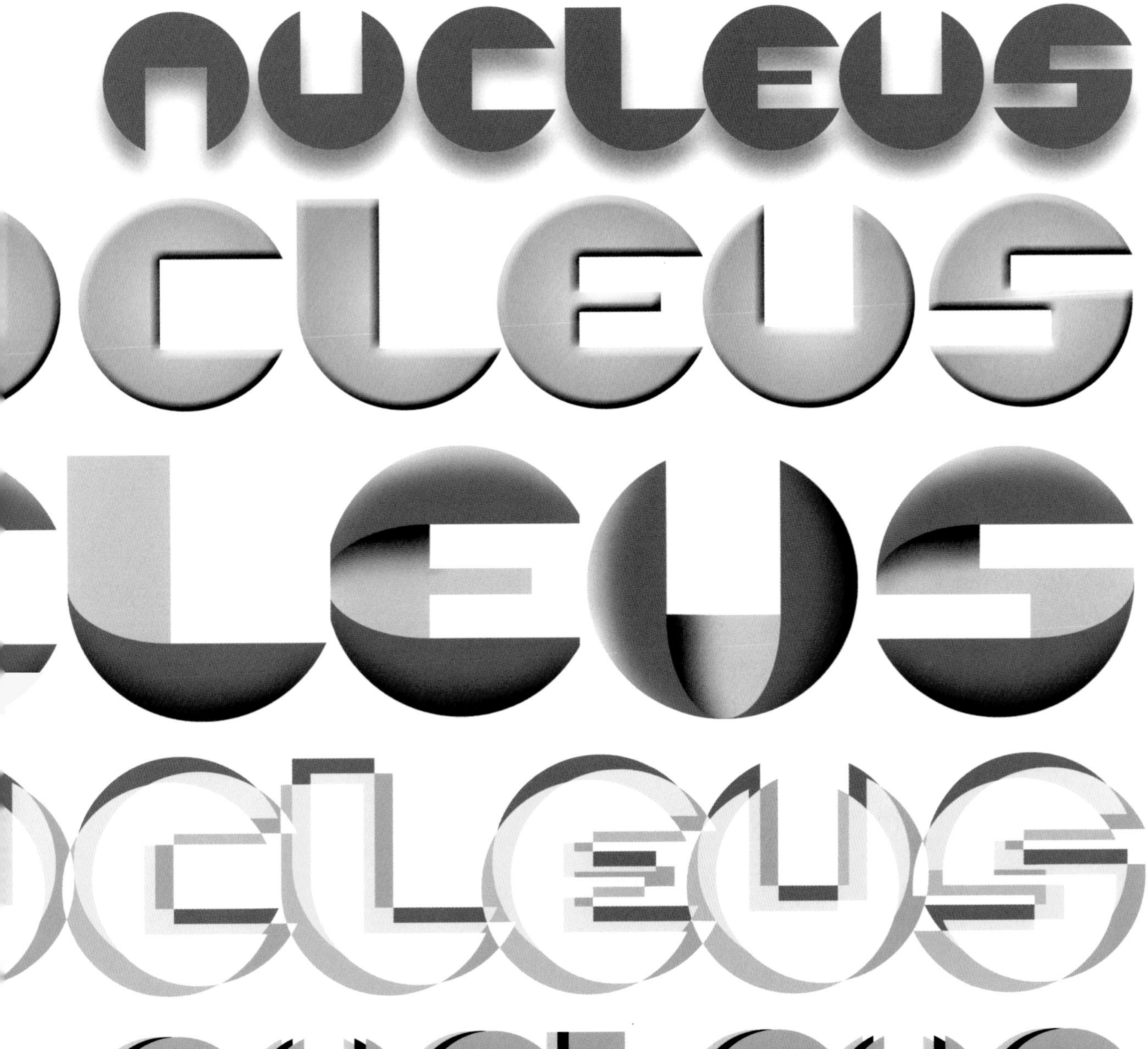

NUCLEUS

NUCLEUS

NUCLEUS

NUCLEUS

NUCLEUS

Besides being symbols to construct a written language,

[letters] can be used to compose any visual impression

imaginable. To me, typography is the visual arrangement

of letterforms and symbols. Its style creates identity.

If a composition contains coherent content, this visual

identity will convey the message in a distinct and

original way. A new expression. A new impression.

A new corner of the mind is opened. How exciting!

Max Kisman

The beauty of a well-designed font goes beyond its ravishingly expressive eyes, its gorgeously sculpted ears and the graceful curves of its necks.* A typeface's real beauty lies in its ability to add to a word's inferences of emotion, personality, behavior and belief. In fact, the perfectly chosen typeface, when placed in the ideal textual context, can convey thematic messages with a precision, conviction and subtlety that even the most well-chosen word might envy. And the charm of a typeface doesn't end there: Typefaces can also exhibit a rascally sense of humor. Take the case of the word *Garamond* being set in Helvetica, or the time when Künstler Script was used to headline a poster for a punk rock show. Talk about wit— it's almost too much for words.

* As any complete diagram of typographic anatomy could tell you, not only do certain letters have eyes, ears and necks, some also have beaks and tails.

Baseline variations

Type usually sits on lines that run straight and level, but it doesn't always have to be that way. Baselines can also curve, bulge, swirl or sag in precise or irregular ways. Another thing that baselines—and ascender lines—can do is act as apparent forces that bend or obscure letters or words (as seen in the first two samples, opposite).

Pay special attention to the spacing between characters when flowing text along curved baselines. The default kerning offered through programs like Illustrator, InDesign and Photoshop is designed to accommodate type set along a straight path, and designers must be willing to adjust the spacing between characters—letter by letter if necessary—when placing text along nonlinear paths.

[A] Illustrator's Warp effects were used to transform this logo's word—along with its horizontal baseline and ascender line—into a perspective-implying design. **[B]** A white ellipse has been used to take a curved bite from the baseline of this logo's bold serif capitals. The letter-blocking shape could also have been wavy, jagged or free-form. **[C]** The characters of this multi-word logo follow a wavy baseline. The expressive qualities of both the flowing baseline and the design's curvaceous ampersand connect well with the meaning of the logo's text. Note how each letter in this design sits perpendicular to its position along the curving baseline. Software controls could also have been used to force all of the letters to stand vertical: Investigate your options when flowing text along any nonlinear, nonhorizontal path. **[D]** The arched baseline of this logo accommodates the placement of the decorative design extending from its capital *A*. The swirls' colored backing adds a subtle note of dimension to the design while also softening the visual step between the dark lines of the swirls and the white page on which they sit.

NUCLEUS

A

BIOTIC

B

whirl, twirl & spin

C

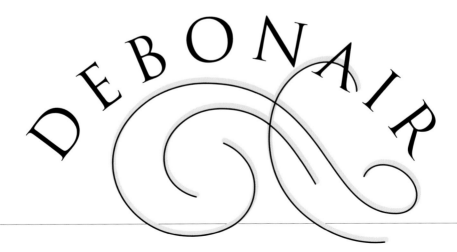

DEBONAIR

D

Alternative baselines

Words may not read as quickly or as easily when presented in nontraditional ways, but as long as they don't strain the eyes or the patience of their target audience, and as long as the aesthetic and thematic gains of the words' presentation are boosted through their alternative means of display, then there's really no reason *not* to consider rule-bending typographic treatments for logos. How about a backward-flowing baseline that forces certain words to read from right to left? What about breaking up a design's baselines—along with the words they support—into multiple parts? Could baselines of various angles be used within a multiword signature? Should vertical baselines be considered, and, if so, should the letters on these baselines flow vertically or should they be stacked one on top of the other?

What other out-of-the-ordinary baseline treatments could be applied to the typography you are working with? How about grabbing a sheet of paper and a pen and brainstorming for ideas using thumbnail sketches?

[A] Arrows and a word that runs backwards along its baseline help emphasize the implications of this logo's words. **[B,C]** Visual intrigue takes precedence over strict readability when words are broken into multiple lines according to a design's compositional needs. The designer must take the preferences of the target audience into account when weighing the pluses and minuses of art vs. practicality issues like this. **[D]** Unless you're trying to come up with a logo that needs to fit on something like a tall industrial smokestack, vertical typographic arrangements are rarely the best bet. Still, that doesn't mean that such arrangements should be automatically ruled out. The letters of this signature have been stacked to fill openings in the DNA-like structure of its icon. **[E]** How about an approach that includes a mix of vertical, horizontal and angled baselines? The surreptitiously positioned *O* at the center of this logo's word acts as the design's point of rotation.

WHIRL
TWIRL
& SPIN

NUCLEUS

[ALLEYCAT]

BIOTIC

DEBONAIR

To enclose or not to enclose

Would an enclosure of some sort improve the thematic and visual presentation of your typographically inclined logo? What about an enclosure that complements the look of your logo's characters? How about an enclosure that provides a note of contrast?

Sometimes an enclosure lends just the right finishing touch to a design, and sometimes a signature's type is better off standing on its own. Which approach is right for the logo you're working on? Use the computer to render a variety of possible solutions and then sit back and let your designer's instinct guide you to the most effective solutions.

[A] This enclosure's halftoned edge gives it a modern look that connects well with the contemporary typography inside. **[B]** An intentionally messy overlapping of elegant decorations lends a look of dissonance to this design—a look that connects nicely with the rough incarnation of its classic serif typeface. **[C]** Ultra-simple lettering paired with an ultra-basic enclosure: Sometimes the most straightforward solutions are also the best. **[D]** A crudely painted stripe serves as a backdrop for crisp sans serif type, which, in turn, provides an enclosure for a casually rendered illustration. **[E]** What about cropping the decorative extensions of your custom-crafted logo with an enclosing shape? **[F,G]** These logos' spacious enclosures do an effective job of claiming additional real estate for designs that would have taken up only a modest amount of compositional territory had they been type-only creations.

1

2

3

[1] A logo's enclosure may closely echo the shape of the material inside. **[2]** An enclosure can also connect with the look of its interior elements more subtly: The arches at the top and bottom of this design are the same that were used in the previous example, only here the arches have been flipped so that they bulge outward. **[3]** What about using an enclosure whose shape contrasts with the logo inside?

A

B

C

D

E

F

G

Exercises

Use the samples throughout The Logo Brainstorm Book *to help generate ideas as you seek solutions for these exercises. Make an effort to push your ideas into fresh creative territory—from thumbnail to finish.*

If you are interested in adding color to any of the designs you create for these exercises, consider checking out chapter 7, Color, pages 268–296, for tips and ideas.

TYPEFACE AS LOGOTYPE

This exercise involves applying typefaces straight from the computer to three different company names. Readers who have access to a large collection of fonts may be able to come up with solutions for each of this exercise's tasks using typefaces that are already on their system. If the font choices on your computer are limited then you might need use typefaces downloaded from the Web (look for free fonts—there are plenty to be found that will work for this exercise).

The challenge here involves coming up with three different type-only logos for each of these company names: Lavender, Granite and Corson Wiley Investments.

* First, present each company name using typefaces that represent the businesses in straightforward corporate terms—as if the target audience were financially secure retirees.

* Some guidelines: Throughout this exercise, you may freely adjust your typography's kerning and line spacing as you see fit and you may also set words as caps, lowercase or as a mix; use a different typeface for each signature you create and make no revisions to any of your chosen fonts' characters (typeface modification will be the focus of the next exercise).

* Next, come up with a second set of presentation-ready typographic logos for the businesses, only this time use typefaces of a casual or funky nature—as though young urban hipster professionals were the intended audience.

* And lastly, do whatever mental gymnastics are necessary to imagine that the three company names you have been working with are actually the names of

three different heavy metal bands and that each band specializes in music of a highly anarchical nature. Your task here is to create a set of type-only designs for the bands by choosing fonts whose visual personalities blatantly contradict any status quo interpretations of the bands' names.

REVISING CHARACTERS

Done with the first exercise? Do you have three sets of type-only logos and does each set contain three ideas? Great. Now it's time to take things a step further (a step that might or might not need to be taken if these logos had been for real-world clients). The task here is to modify some or all of the letters in three of your designs so that each signature assumes a typographic identity that's clearly different than before.

• Select one signature from each of your sets of typographic logos.

• Convert the characters in the three signatures to paths (a preemptive step that's almost always necessary prior to exploring typeface modifications).

• Begin considering ways of modifying the look of each signature. Here are a few ideas: Add decorative or visually expressive extensions to one or more letters, link or combine characters in interesting ways, modify the serifs or endpoints of the logos' letters, fill characters with a pattern or an image or apply digital effects.

• Look through the pages of this chapter for more character-altering ideas: Any kind of letter-modifying treatment that comes to mind is fair game.

CUSTOM-MADE TYPOGRAPHY

Your client, Aperture Photo Finishing, has asked for a custom-crafted type-only logo design. (Actually, they've asked that the word *Aperture* be custom made specifically for this project—*Photo Finishing* could be custom or it could be set using an existing typeface).

• The client prefers relatively precise, geometrically inclined letterforms, but that's not to say that they aren't open to a little stylistic flair.

• The logo's letters may subtly convey aspects of photography, but the client is equally open to a signature that simply comes across as clean, creative, forward thinking and professional. Knowing this, feel free to add pictorial elements to the design, but keep in mind that the client has stated their preference for a typographic signature: Keep any icons or images small and subtle.

- Consider basing your letterforms on one or two basic geometric or free-form shapes (see the bottom of page 180 for more about this letter-forming strategy.)
- Aim for a consistent look among your characters in terms of their weight, spacing, style and proportions.
- Link characters or add letterform extensions if you feel that modifications such as these will enhance the look of your signature.
- Caps, lowercase or a mix of uppercase and lowercase letters may be used.

WORDS AS IMAGES AND VICE VERSA

Designers often need reminding that not all their creative work has to be thought of in commercial terms and with a client's expectations in mind. This exercise is meant to serve as just such a reminder while giving you a chance to temporarily set aside your money-making and client-pleasing mind-set and to have some good old-fashioned creative fun. (And for those of you who are especially career-driven in your creative pursuits, rest assured that the lessons learned in this exercise can—and almost certainly will—come in handy for future design jobs.)

The project here is to construct a word that looks like a picture (or a picture that looks like a word—if you'd rather look at it that way). The rules for this one are few:

- Choose a word and then render it in such a way that the word's meaning is visually conveyed through the presentation of its letters.
- The word's letters could come from a typeface or they could be custom-rendered. Illustrations, images, ornamentation and icons may be used.
- Your goal is to come up with a design that sits about halfway between the realms of word and image.
- The signature on pages 174–175 is an example of this kind of signature, but it is only one way of handling this kind of design challenge. Brainstorm for unique

solutions that reflect your personal tastes and stylistic preferences.

CURVING BASELINES AND CUSTOM KERNING

The longest nontechnical, noncoined word in the English language is *antidisestablishmentarianism.* A pretty good choice, wouldn't you say, for a study of kerning? And, just to make this kerning challenge a bit more ... *challenging* ... how about flowing the word's letters along a nonlinear baseline?

• Use a program like Illustrator or InDesign to typeset the word *antidisestablishmentarianism* in whatever font you like.

• The word may be set in caps, in lowercase or as a mix.

• Attach the word to a curved baseline. The baseline could be arched, circular, wavy, spiraling or free-form.

• Next, set about the task of manually kerning the characters of this mega-letter monstrosity. Keep the overall kerning of the word slightly tighter than normal and aim for a high level of letterspacing consistency throughout.

• Know that achieving consistent kerning in a case like this is a greater challenge than it might first appear, and that time and patience will come into play as you fine tune this word's pairs and sets of letters. One excellent way to evaluate kerning is to sit back from the computer from time to time and to look at a word's letters in sets of three: Compare trios of consecutive letters from throughout the word and aim for letterspacing that is as alike as possible between each of the sets. Another useful evaluation strategy is to squint your eyes until a word begins to appear out of focus—this trick often reveals portions of a word that appear visually darker (indicating portions of the word that are kerned more tightly than the standard you are aiming for) or lighter (areas that are too loosely kerned).

5   Type + Symbol

CHAPTER CONTENTS

5   Type + Symbol

ARE YOU WORKING ON A LOGO that's a combination of an icon (an abstract or pictorial symbol or a monogram) and one or more words of type? If so, then at some point you'll need to look for ways of combining your logo's elements into a cohesive and attractive compositional unit. Before you get to that, however, you'll need to decide which to work on first, the signature's symbol or its type.

Most of the time, designers choose to come up with ideas for a signature's symbol before looking for ways of presenting its type. One reason for this is that symbols tend to be the theme-setting focal points of signatures, and it's only after the symbol has been designed (at least in rough form) that it becomes apparent which fonts—and what sorts of typographic arrangements

and treatments—will best complete the logo's mission of presenting itself effectively through strong aesthetics and on-target thematic conveyances.

This doesn't mean that all typographic considerations should be put on hold while working on a symbol: Good designers are always keeping their eyes and mind open to upcoming typographic possibilities when developing an icon, and they often switch back and forth between finalizing the look of a logo's symbol and the presentation of its type in order to come up with just the right connection between the two.

Also, know that there is no hard-and-fast rule that demands that a logo's signature be developed before type is added to it.

If your project seems to be calling for another approach—that of developing the logo's typographic elements first, or one that calls for creating the type and symbolic elements more or less simultaneously—then by all means, work in whatever manner seems best.

The samples in this chapter have been built using symbols and monograms from chapters 2 and 3. Type has been added to these abstract, pictorial and letter-based symbols in order to produce the signatures on the pages ahead. Use these samples as brainstorm material and as springboards to presentation-worthy designs that are entirely your own.

Relativity

First and foremost, when you are investigating ways of combining a company's name with its icon, take a good look at the relationships that are occurring between the two. Does the font visually and thematically echo the look and feel of the icon? Should there be a harmonious connection between the two, or should the font and the icon be allowed to thematically disagree in order to convey divergent themes? What about the size of the icon compared with the size of the type? Which should dominate, and by how much? What about spatial relationships? Should the icon sit above, below or alongside the type? Would a symmetrical or an asymmetrical arrangement suit the project best? How much space should there be between the signature's type and its icon? What would happen if the type and icon overlapped? Should the type be black while the icon is colored, or should it be the other way around? Enough questions for now: Time to start brainstorming the options.

theCle

Small typography centered above large icon

Typography to left of icon

Typography to the right of icon

Icon

theCleverCat

erCat the

theCleverCat

Type centered below icon

theCleverCat

Typography centered well beneath icon

203

Tried-and-true configurations

It's common to see signatures arranged with an icon sitting above, below or alongside a company's name. These are practical arrangements that lend themselves nicely to things like letterheads, web mastheads and packaging designs. And, just because arrangements like these are common, it doesn't mean they should be ruled out as boring or status quo: Any aesthetically sound pairing between an eye-catching icon and well-executed typography stands a good chance of serving as an effective and attractive signature.

[A] A centered arrangement of icon, logotype and subtext. **[B]** Another tried-and-true option: icon to the left of typography. **[C]** Positioning an icon to the right of a logo's type is a less common arrangement, though certainly worth considering. **[D]** Here, the signature's icon—because it is a functioning typographic element as well—is placed within the two words of the company's name. See pages 219–223 for more examples of icons that also function as letters. **[E]** How about a decidedly off-centered arrangement of your logo's components? The up-and-to-the-right expression generated by the placement and the slanting construction of this signature's icon is counterbalanced by the anchoring gesture of the enlarged *M* at the far left of the design.

When placing an icon alongside type, consider a variety of size and position options. Should the symbol be the same vertical height as the type's capitals? Should it extend above the typography's cap height and/or below its baseline? How close should the icon be to the type? Which compositional choices produce the best looking and the most practical arrangement?

Mountain Water Lodge
at June Lake

A

WALTERS

B

RowdyJenkinsBlogWorld.com

C

good&bad

D

MAXFIELD

E

205

Other straightforward arrangements

Combining an icon with a multiword company name? If so, be sure to spend time looking for ways of arranging the words and the icon into a neat compositional unit. Explore ideas that involve one size of type as well as solutions that involve two or more font sizes. Investigate symmetrical and asymmetrical compositions and try out arrangements that grant different degrees of visual impact to the signature's elements. Should alterations be made to the type (such as curving some or all of its baselines) to create space for the icon? How about inserting the icon between two words? What about sticking with a no-nonsense arrangement such as an icon centered above center-aligned type?

[A] How about sandwiching your logo's pictorial element between words? The letterforms at the top of this signature have been customized to allow their baselines to stay clear of the illustration's elliptical footprint. Designers must often make modifications to a logo's letters—in either subtle or obvious ways—to adapt them to the compositional needs of a design. **[B]** What about enclosing your signature's components with lines? (More enclosure ideas are presented in chapter 6, Emblems, pages 240–267). **[C,D]** When combining two or more words with a symbol, look for arrangements that provide a convenient space for the icon. Take advantage of the flexibility and speed offered through software and investigate many options: Explore solutions that feature words of the same point size as well as arrangements that make use of more than one size of type; try arranging your words flush left, flush right, centered, justified or none of the above. **[E,F]** The first of these two samples incorporates a symbol that originally appeared on page 39. The second features a reproportioned version of the icon. Note how the second rendition of the signature grants increased visual attention to the symbol while decreasing the vertical reach of the design. Neither approach is superior to the other: This comparison is intended as a reminder to try out all kinds of compositional alternatives before deciding on the most attractive and functional way of finalizing a logo's components.

CARLOTE
VINYARDS

SANJURO
S
STEELWORKS

the
Sontani
Foundation

Cardinal
Conservation
Habitat Management and Preservation

ENCLOSURE
INTERIORS

ENCLOSURE
INTERIORS

A | B

C | D

E | F

Visual echoes

Looking for a typographic mate for the symbol you've created? Begin by taking a good look at the icon. What are its defining characteristics? Is it tall and skinny? Short and wide? Is it made up of thin lines? Is it built from bold shapes? Is it serious, silly, sleek, minimalist or complex? Is it geometric and precise or is it made from casual and free-form shapes?

Once you've got a handle on your icon's visual personality and are ready to play matchmaker between symbol and font, you must first answer this question: Should the pairing be made according to visual and thematic likenesses, or should the union be based on the notion that opposites attract? This spread and the next feature samples and commentary related to both kinds of compositional couplings.

[A] Old meets new: This signature's icon is a blend of classic realism and modern simplification; its typeface is a mix of traditional inline styling and contemporary coloring. **[B]** The type and icon of this design harmoniously relate through their modern and horizontally stretched presentation. A pleasing amount of contrast has also been generated by pairing a smoothly rendered icon with a digitally corrupted typeface. **[C]** The thin lines and minimalist overtones of this signature's icon connect both thematically and literally with the austere and compressed forms of the sans serif font below it. The traditional serif font used to complete the design rounds off the signature's conveyances by suggesting that there is more to these luxury suites than understated simplicity and sophisticated restraint.

Interested in generating a sense of visual tension and thematic depth through your signature? How about intentionally choosing a font that contrasts with the style of your icon? (See the next spread for more ideas along these lines.)

A

B C

Intentional contrast

Contrast is the aim of the type + symbol associations on this spread: These visual partnerships have agreed to disagree for the sake of promoting thematic nuances of diversity and depth. For example, take a look at sample **[C]**. What we have here is a beauty-and-the-beast union between an ornately rendered icon and a weather-beaten set of bold sans serif capitals. It's an appealing fusion of opposites that, in human terms, might be akin to a range-riding cowboy who also happens to excel as a ballroom dancer.

When should a designer seek harmonious relationships between type and icon? When should contrast be the goal? That all depends on the preferences of the designer, the tastes of the client and the kinds of conveyances being sought in order to reach the target audience. When preparing to present ideas to a client, consider offering designs of both types—harmonious and discordant. That way, you can discuss the merits of each while deciding which approach is most advantageous for the project at hand.

[A] What about infusing your signature with connotations of artful sophistication by pairing a modernist graphic with a font of hand-lettered calligraphic characters? **[B]** Here, a typeface made of precise forms has been paired with a pattern of slightly irregular triangles. The result is a signature that seems to suggest that the business being represented is one that has found a workable alliance between accountable business practices and creative freedom. **[C]** Conveyances of modernity can be delivered by audaciously fusing a gracefully rendered icon with visually corrupt letterforms (or vice versa). Stylistic juxtapositions of this kind are a way of broad-casting multifaceted suggestions of fashionable complexity. **[D]** Both the icon and typeface in this signature are geometrically rendered and modern. A sense of diversity enters the picture through the pairing of a highly vertical typeface with a symbol of overtly broad proportions. **[E]** How about generating hints of insurgency and rebellion (either playfully or in earnest) by rendering your logo's typographic elements right across the face of its rigorously drawn icon in a graffiti-like manner?

Terrace Townhomes

A

GIOVANTI FABRICS

B

CONQUERER

C

SIPPOT

D

insight

E

Pre-presentation playtime

You've spent hours, days or weeks coming up with three or four icons that are ready for presentation. Now you've narrowed down the font choices for the company's name and are looking for ideal compositional relationships between your icons and the signature's type. Before you go any further, try this: Relax. Sit back and relish the knowledge that you have good-looking icons "in the bank" and several intriguing typographic choices to choose from. The pressure is relieved, and now it's time to freely and creatively explore solutions that range from conventional to outlandish.

A tip: Search far and wide during this exploratory stage. Push the bounds of normalcy. Go *too* far— and then pull back as necessary. Come up with at least a half dozen options for each icon that you plan on presenting to the client before deciding which ones to actually bring to the table. (And be sure to save some of your unused designs on your laptop so that you can let the client have a look if your presentation seems to be drifting in the direction of one of your alternate ideas.)

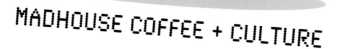

A conclusion is the
place where you got tired
of thinking.

Steven Wright

There are three responses
to a piece of design—
yes, *no* and WOW!
Wow is the one to aim for.

Milton Glaser

How do you know when you're finished coming up with logo ideas for a presentation? Is it when your attention span expires or when you have a lukewarm feeling in your gut that suggests that you can probably think up a convincing argument for at least one of your designs? Or, on the other hand, is it when you have not one, but three or four ideas that you are so crazy about—so excited to present—that your biggest worry is over how the client will possibly be able to choose between such cleverly conceived and exquisitely rendered candidates? Obviously, it's the latter, and unless a truly unreasonable deadline forces the issue, don't ever put a project to rest until you feel properly ecstatic over its prospects for success.

Typographic extensions

Consider creating a seamless visual link between your signature's icon and its typography. You could begin a logo project with this compositional strategy in mind, or you could start looking for ways of connecting type with symbol after you have developed one or more stand-alone icons. Either way, be sure to explore font-choice options along the way: Should your font relate harmoniously with the icon or should it provide a measure of contrast? Which route produces the most visually and thematically effective result?

[A] The forms of many letters can be extended in ways that connect with—or transform into—anything from a simple flourish to a complex icon. **[B]** The dot on the *i* in this signature's type also serves as an element within its icon. Designers take note: The dot of the lowercase *i* and *j* possess an inherent potential for all kinds of visual and thematic opportunity. **[C]** Though separated by a narrow gap, the linear forms of this company's icon connect clearly with the typeface below it. Look at the letters of your client's name, and at the icon you are designing for them, and ask yourself whether visual connections between the two could—and should—be considered.

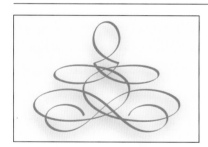

If you've created a stand-alone icon, and then decide to merge it with a typographic element, be willing to spend time making adjustments to the icon and the type so that the two can gracefully meld. For example, the icon used for the "pranayama" signature on this spread was first featured as a self-contained symbol on page 109. In order to join the symbol and the type, a simple typographic extension (circled above) had to be added to the signature's lowercase *y* in order to link it with the icon.

A

B

C

Custom characters

hexe

Here's another example of an icon that's an extension of type, only this time the font being used is custom built. Font creation is an art of its own, but that doesn't mean all letters require great skill to create. The simple, geometric characters of this signature were produced quickly and without difficulty: A Helvetica version of the word was placed in an Illustrator document, an empty layer was added over top and the PEN tool was used to draw ultra-geometric letterforms using the Helvetica characters as proportional guides. How about a custom-crafted font for the signature you're working on? If you have the skills to create the characters yourself, great. Otherwise, how about hiring a freelance type designer?

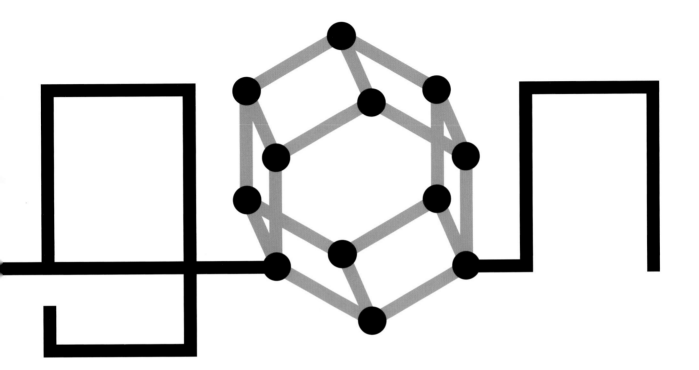

Letter enhancement and replacement

The letter-impersonating icons shown on this spread act as substitutes for characters within company names. The resulting signatures are both typographic and pictorial, and even though the icons are part of the typography, each could also serve as a stand-alone symbol.

Legibility is the primary concern when creating signatures like these. Be sure that the design of your icon/letter doesn't interfere with the readability of the word(s) they are part of. Naturally, the safest solutions are those that involve a pictorial symbol that closely resembles the form of the character being replaced. Still, you may be surprised at what you can get away with in this regard. For example, note that even though the car in sample **[D]** only vaguely resembles a capital *A*, the word reads well—probably because the image of the car gives the brain a clear idea as to what word is being processed.

[A] A bold and extended character was used for the first letter of this company's name—a character with enough internal space to house a thematically relevant illustration. **[B]** The expressive legs of this signature's human-referencing icon do a fair job of imitating a lowercase *n*. The dynamic forms of the logo's openface font lend additional inferences of animation to the design. **[C]** Is there a way of using an icon to bridge a gap between the words of your client's name? **[D]** The connotations of playfulness and action generated by this signature's icon are amplified through its juxtaposition with a stolid row of bold sans serif capitals. **[E]** Here, the letter *X* has been replaced by a dynamically rendered icon built from layers of translucent free-form shapes. The artful and decorative qualities of this logo's icon contrast nicely with the sensibly rendered characters of its classic serif font.

Peekaboo

A

dancePants

B

SOUND CONTROL

C

QUICKCAR

D

AXIOM

E

Letter replacement: *O* and *Q*

Generally speaking, the letter *O* is more easily replaced with pictorial material than other characters. One reason for this is that it's easier to create an icon that fits within a circular or elliptical footprint than it is to design a symbol that conforms to the shape of something like a capital *G* or a lowercase *a*. Another reason the letter *O* is so easily replaced by pictorial matter is that the eye tends to accept a variety of symmetrical shapes—including squares, diamonds and stars—as reasonable replacements for this character. Does the name of your client contain an *O* (or possibly a *Q*)? If so, do you think the client would mind if you replaced it with an icon?

[A] Got an *O* in the signature you're working on? How about converting it into a decorative frame and filling it with a photo or an illustration? **[B]** This logo's *o* has been replaced by a colored circle that serves as a backdrop for an illustrative icon. **[C]** Remember, a letter-replacing icon need not necessarily mimic the exact shape of the character it represents. **[D]** This circular icon has been paired with an ultra narrow font for the sake of visual contrast. (Other pairings are considered below.) **[E]** How about introducing a subtle hint of whimsy to your otherwise austere signature? The floating globe in this design does just that—while also demonstrating the meaning of the word it is part of. **[F]** The thin and geometric forms of this font are paired with a stylistically contrasting *Q* made from hand-drawn circles and a bold rectangular tail.

Sample **[D]** on the opposite page features a contrasting pairing between an ultra-condensed typeface and a perfectly round icon. Here, a more visually harmonious relationship has been achieved by using a sans serif font of normal proportions.

How about exploring other options? What about bracketing the icon between a pair of capital letters? In this sample, a serif face contrasts nicely against the sans serif nature of the circular icon.

What about a contemporary monospaced font whose similar-width characters have qualities of both serif and sans serif typefaces? The point of these three samples is to serve as a reminder to explore multiple solutions to any design challenge.

Alternative Automobile Fuels

TECHNOLOGIES

Lexic**o**n

ACCOUNT MANAGEMENT

A | B

C | D

E | F

223

Type within and among icons

A major concern in the graphic arts—whenever a word is placed over a backdrop—is to ensure that the backdrop does not interfere with the type's readability. This is especially true for signatures since one of the main functions of a logo is to quickly and clearly convey the name of the company it represents.

That said, there is some wiggle room when it comes the legibility of the type in signatures—particularly when it comes to logos that are aimed at younger audiences: Youthful eyes tend to be more accepting of visual challenges than the eyes of older viewers. (Conduct a few side-by-side comparisons of logos found in a skateboarding magazine with logos featured in a business journal and you'll see the truth in this assertion.)

Several more type-over-icon design strategies are presented on the next spread.

[A] What about designing an icon that can be used as a stand-alone visual *and* as a backdrop for the client's name? **[B]** This signature's roughly rendered and blurred letterforms run right through the middle of its icon. A subtle white glow has been added around the type to help it stand apart from the symbol below it (more type-over-icon design strategies are presented on the next spread). **[C]** Is there a light and plain area of your icon that could serve as a noninterfering backdrop for the signature's type? **[D]** The antlers of the odd-looking creature in this signature connect with the logo's type by way of overlap. Take whatever measures are necessary to ensure the readability of a signature's words when crafting logos like this. **[E]** How about a vertical baseline? Should the word read upwards or downwards? **[F]** When designing for a forward-thinking client and their contemporary-minded audience, legibility can be pushed toward its limit. Here, a signature's typographic elements have been set over a photograph in a way that challenges readability without quite defeating it.

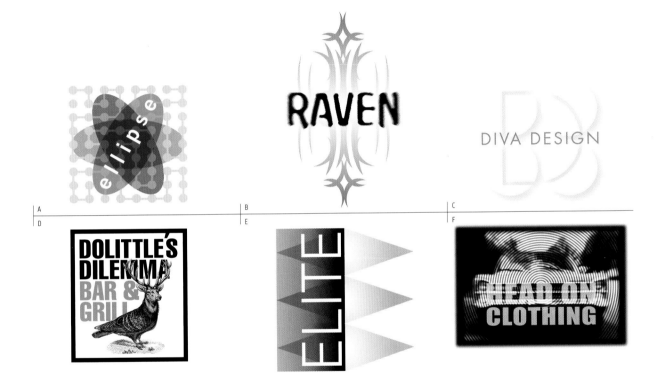

A   B   C
D   E   F

Overlapping strategies

Safeguarding the readability of type as it crosses over or through an image is a task designers regularly grapple with when creating ads, posters, business cards, websites and logos. The purpose of this spread is to offer a look at ten possible solutions to this kind of oft-encountered design challenge. The approaches demonstrat- ed here are not the only ways of resolving issues that arise when images and letters cross paths, but they do represent a core of effective compositional strategies that could be considered when handling readability issues. (How about bookmarking this spread? You may find it helpful the next time you're working on a project that involves type that overlaps an image.)

KillYourTelevision.com

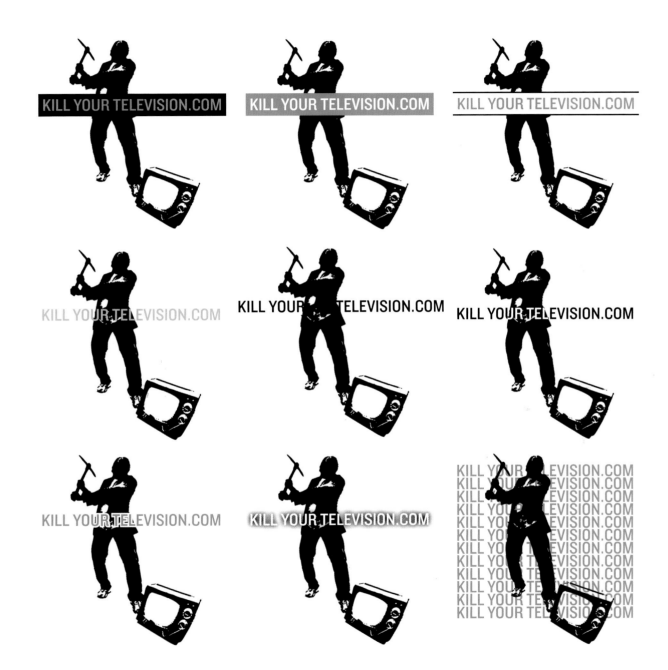

227

In the name of God, stop a moment,

cease your work, look around you.

Leo Tolstoy

Be culturally literate, because if you

don't have any understanding

of the world you live in and the culture

you live in, you're not going to express

anything to anybody else.

Paula Scher

To produce effective work, designers must gain a clear understanding of their target audience's beliefs, assumptions and experiences before attempting to connect with them through graphic symbols. For instance, a designer might wisely choose a classically rendered calligraphic depiction of a tidal wave as an icon for a company that produces handmade sumi brushes, but would that same tidal wave be an appropriate choice for a hotel located on tsunami-prone beachfront property? Probably not. Step back from your sketch pad or computer from time to time and take stock of the situation: Are you working with an accurate and in-depth understanding of how the members of your target audience view the world? If not, then it's time to get better acquainted with them through whatever means necessary.

Alternate realities

maybe, in the real world, there is no giant pink tower waiting to serve milkshakes to happy customers. But what if there was? Or what if we pretended there was, and what if Photoshop were used to create a signature that portrayed this unlikely fiction as hard fact?

This reality-twisting notion is offered here—sandwiched as it is between spreads that deal with more down-to-earth design solutions—as a way of introducing a question: What if you were to alter your conceptual focus for a few minutes and consider a few "out there" ideas as you brainstorm for eye-catching solutions for your logo project?

Mayberry Milkshake Co.

Typographic enclosures

Type doesn't always have to follow a straight and horizontal line. What about wrapping your icon with type that follows the shape of a circle, square, triangle or ellipse? Programs like Illustrator and Photoshop have tools that allow designers to apply type to nonhorizontal baselines, as well as a generous set of type-enhancing features that can be used to alter the kerning, size and leading of a signature's words. (When placing letters along a circular or elliptical path, pay special attention to kerning—default kerning is primarily intended for characters that flow along a horizontal baseline.)

When creating a shaped enclosure with type, consider accompanying the type with linework that helps separate it from the logo's illustrative elements. Also, think about using areas of color to emphasize a signature's overall shape as well as to provide a backdrop for reversed or overprinting type.

See chapter 6, Emblems, pages 240–267, for expansions of the visual themes presented here.

[A] A circular enclosure of type and color. For the sake of emphasis, the two words at the top of this design have been featured in a slightly heavier face than the logo's subtext. [B] Type, and type alone, forms this signature's circular enclosure. The two-baseline structure of this logo allows its type to appear right-side-up at the circle's top and bottom while the continuous baseline of the previous design causes the text to appear upside down at its bottom: Consider both baseline options when flowing text around a circle. [C] What about filling a noncircular enclosure with type? How about designing your signature based on the form of a triangle, square, rectangle, diamond, polygon or ellipse? What about a free-form shape? [D] The roughly rendered type in this retro-yet-contemporary logo echoes the look of its illustrative components as it follows the design's elliptical perimeter. [E] A bold border of repeating typographic elements frame this signature's icon. Given the name of the organization being represented, it makes sense that this logo's words should be joined closely with each other and with the design's icon.

A

B

C

D

E

233

Framing

Compositional framing involves using components of a design to enclose or bracket another component. Framing helps direct viewers' attention while lending a sense of cohesion to a signature. How about enclosing a logo's typography between elements of a multipart icon? What about bracketing an icon between letters or words? Consider solutions that are symmetrical and asymmetrical, horizontal and vertical, commonplace and unusual.

[A] Though originally designed as a one-part icon (see page 53), the symbol used in this signature seems to express itself best when mirrored above and below this company's name. **[B]** What about using type to bracket a symbol? This logo's icon has been placed in a gap between two of the signature's words. The filigree behind the bee provides a useful visual connector between this logo's icon and its type. **[C]** Be open to making changes to your icon when adding typographic elements. The shadow below the sheet of paper in this icon (first featured on page 53) was lowered when it was decided that an effective design could be created by framing the logo's type between the paper and its shadow.

What about trying a different approach as you search for ways of adding type to an icon? What about creating a complex multidimensional emblem? And how about leaving out your icon completely and going with a type-only solution? If either of these creative routes seem worth looking into, check out chapter 6, Emblems, pages 240–267, or chapter 4, Typographic Logos, pages 154–195.

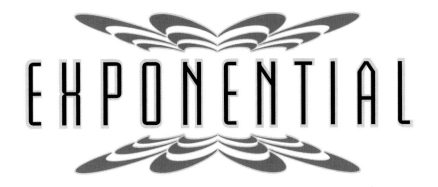

EXPONENTIAL

A

The Beautiful Bee

B

Tennenbaum

ACCOUNTING

C

Exercises

Use the samples throughout The Logo Brainstorm Book *to help generate ideas as you seek solutions for these exercises. Make an effort to push your ideas into fresh creative territory—from thumbnail to finish.*

If you are interested in adding color to any of the designs you create for these exercises, consider checking out chapter 7, Color, pages 268–296, for tips and ideas.

Note: You will need to use icons or monograms created for the exercises at the end of chapters 2 and 3 for several of this chapter's projects.

CENTERED VARIATIONS

A client who strongly favors centered visual arrangements is in need of a new signature. Your job is to produce three presentation-worthy designs—each of which is to be compositionally centered, and each of which is to look notably different than the others.

- Begin this project by coming up with a company name that can be combined with an icon or a monogram that you created for an exercise at the end of either chapter 2 or chapter 3. Choose a one-word company name for this project.

- Look for and select several typefaces that could be used for your signature's type. (Feel free to change your mind and to try out other typefaces once the project gets going.)

- Your three designs should each use a different typeface and each signature should convey a visual personality that is distinctly its own.

- Seek centered arrangements between your signature's icon or monogram and its type. See what happens when the icon or monogram is positioned above and below the type at different distances and at different sizes. Is there a way of placing the icon behind the type?

- Consider making modifications to the forms of the signature's letters and to the look of its icon or monogram as you work—do whatever it takes to come up with attractive compositions.

- Be sure to investigate designs that grant different levels of visual strength to the signature's components. Should the icon dominate? Should the type stand out most? How much contrast should there be between the two? Try out many different solutions before deciding which three designs work best.

- Linework and simple enclosures are permissible.

CULTIVATING CONTRAST

Here, your job is to come up with three signatures that are strong on contrast and asymmetry. Aim for a set of designs that would make for an exceptionally strong presentation to a contemporary-minded client.

- Choose a symbol or a monogram that you created for one of the exercises in chapter 2 or chapter 3.

- Come up with a company name to go with your symbol or monogram. The name should have two, three or four words.

- Find a few typefaces that visually contrast with the look of your symbol or monogram (see pages 210–211 for more on the topic of type vs. icon contrast). Use these fonts as your starter selection and add or subtract from the set as your ideas develop.

- Begin exploring asymmetrical arrangements between your signatures' typographic and pictorial components (samples **[C]** and **[D]** on page 207 are good examples of asymmetrical signature designs).

- Thoroughly explore variations in the arrangement of your signatures' elements, as well as differences in the sizing and spacing of their components.

- Linework and enclosures may be used, and color may be added to the designs.

- Aim for outcomes that are sassy, sophisticated, unconventional, humorous, cutting edge or all of the above.

ENCLOSING WITH TYPE

This assignment involves finding three attractive and compositionally effective ways of enclosing a symbol or monogram with type. A few specific project requirements are mentioned in the text that follows.

- Choose a multiword company name to use with a symbol or monogram from one of the exercises at the end of chapter 2 or chapter 3.

- Start exploring ways of enclosing your symbol or monogram with the multiword company name.

- Two of your signatures should feature type that completely surrounds its symbol or monogram. The type in the third design should only partly enclose the symbol or monogram.

- Each design should use a different typeface and any design may employ more than one typeface.

- Come up with at least one signature that uses type that contrasts with its symbol or monogram.

- Produce at least one design that employs type that harmoniously connects with its symbol or monogram.

- Aim for a different overall shape for each design: rectangular, triangular, elliptical, free-form, etc.

- Linework may be used and colors may be applied.

Tip: When placing type on a curved baseline (as when setting type in a circle), pay special attention to kerning:

Make adjustments as needed to produce consistent spacing among each of the word's letters.

JOINING LETTERS WITH ICONS

You won't need to use any previously created symbols or monograms for this exercise; here, you will be working for a hi-tech firm named Radiance and your task is to create, from scratch, a signature whose type and icon compositionally interact (see pages 216–223 for examples of this kind of logo).

- Brainstorm for icon ideas and make plenty of thumbnail sketches to get ideas going. Your goal is to come up with an abstract or representational symbol that connotes aspects of technology and communication, and then to find a way of visually connecting this icon with the company's name.

- Linework, enclosures and color may be applied to the design.

LETTER REPLACEMENT

This exercise is more for fun and creative exploration than it is for impressing a would-be client.

- Begin by applying a basic serif or sans serif font to the words *highway*, *anger* and *sunflower*. The words may be typed as all caps, in lowercase or as a mix.

- Now, replace one of the letters in each word with a custom-created icon, ornament, doodle, illustration, pattern or photo that bears some kind of connection with the word's meaning.

- Do not let your alterations interfere with legibility.

- Strive for nonobvious solutions that are uniquely conceived and attractively rendered.

- Need examples? See pages 219–223.

PHOTO PLAY

Got a digital camera? And do you posses at least a basic understanding of Photoshop's tools and treatments? If so, this project is designed to give you the opportunity to freely explore ways of incorporating type into photos— and its lessons may come in handy the next time you're looking for an intriguing way of producing an icon or an illustration using text and imagery.

- Begin by selecting three or four photos of interest from your personal cache (either that, or head out during lunchtime and capture a few intriguing photos from your surroundings).

- With your three or four photos in front of you, think of a word that could be used to label each image in a humorous or thought-provoking way.

- Next, explore ways of bringing your word into its assigned photo using Photoshop tools and treatments. The word could be integrated into a specific part of the image (added to the side of a bus, for instance), it could be placed into a relatively blank area of the picture or it could be printed right across the face of the image. And what about special effects? Could these be used to help your word stand out from its photographic surroundings? Use whatever Photoshop skills you have and explore and experiment until you are pleased with your results.

(And when you're done, how about making a mini-gallery of your creations by hanging them on a nearby wall?)

6   Emblems

CHAPTER CONTENTS

6 Emblems

ELABORATE EMBLEMS aren't the answer to all commercial branding projects, but, when the chance to produce one does arise, it could be time for a small workplace celebration: Rare is the designer who would not leap at the chance to develop one of these intricate and colorful constructions of letters, images, patterns, decorations and bordering elements. After all, what is there for designers *not* to get excited about when called upon to develop a piece of art that might include just about every kind of visual element that drew them to their profession in the first place?

Whether you are aiming for an emblem that is bursting with visual energy, a creation that's sleek and minimal or

243

something in between, give focused attention to each of your design's elements. Explore variations to the composition's exterior shape, see how things look with—and without— added linework, try out a variety of typefaces and typographic arrangements, investigate various levels of visual hierarchy, experiment with different placements for the emblem's components and look at different ways of finishing things off with decorative patterns, ornamentation and special effects.

Much is possible when designing with such a rich assortment of artistic possibilities, and with all that there is to consider when assembling an emblem, it becomes more important than ever to begin the creative process by thoroughly brainstorming for visual and thematic building blocks before the actual computer-based logo construction begins: Start by coming up with lists of potential subject matter (see pages 17–19 for more about brainstorming with lists), make plenty of thumbnail sketches (covered beginning on page 22) to explore possible arrangements of components and use this chapter's content to spark stylistic, thematic and visual avenues of exploration.

Construction considerations

Emblem-like logos can be built by constructing visual enclosures around words, symbols, mono-grams, illustrations and photos. The look of an enclosure plays a major role in the stylistic and thematic conveyances of a design, and its form is as worthy of consideration as any of the elements it will hold. When beginning work on an emblem, be sure to spend time considering different ways of enclosing the design. Should the enclosure present itself in simple geometric terms or should it take on a more complex and free-form visual expression? Should the enclosure have separate panels for things like type, images and decorative elements? Would it be best if the enclosure echoed the look of the design's other components or should it contrast with them? Could the enclosure be designed to attract attention through strong colors and bold shapes, or would it be better to play down its presence? And what about style? Modern, traditional, funky, minimalist, maximalist? Turn to this spread the next time you begin work on an emblem and meld its ideas with inspiration from other pages and other sources as you develop your design's enclosure.

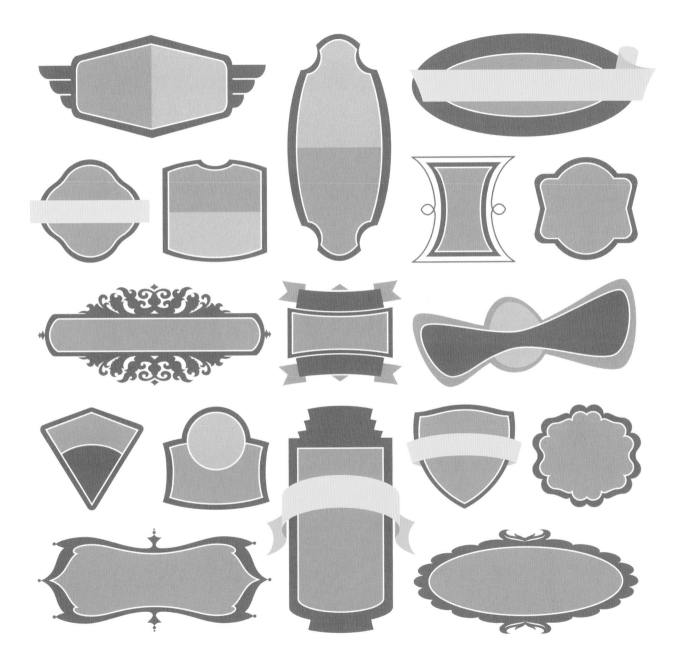

Enclosures from basic shapes

Emblems offer designers the chance to consider all kinds of visual elements, the opportunity to explore a huge range of thematic expressions and an opening to investigate endless stylistic outcomes. This spread features a set of relatively straightforward designs that have been developed from simple geometric or free-form shapes. The styles presented in this batch of emblems range from contemporary to retro, from elegant to casual, and from festive to scholarly. The look of some of the logos has remained simple from start to finish. The presentation of others has evolved into complex creations that feature multiple colors, depth-implying shading, decorative patterns, ornate add-ons and eye-catching type. Edge treatments (such as the scallops around the circumference of **[A]**) have been applied to some of the samples, linework has been used in others, special effects have been applied to several and a graphically rendered banner has been strung across the front of one of the designs.

[A] A basic round enclosure with a traditional scalloped edge. The other samples on this spread tend toward more visually active solutions—which isn't to suggest that there's anything wrong with a simple design like this. **[B]** Even though this logo's elements largely ignore the boundaries of their circular backdrop, the shaded circle still acts as an effective composition-binding enclosure. **[C]** This emblem's strong lines, bold colors, prominent symbol and classic all-cap typography work in concert to present a look that is as festive as it is confident and authoritative. **[D]** What about a freely shaped enclosure? Something that's neither square, circular or triangular? And how about filling the enclosure with perspective-obeying type and shading the entire design dimensionally? **[E]** A contemporary assemblage of type. Thick linework and a strong use of color take an otherwise mundane business name and address and present them to the world in an eye-catching way. **[F]** An elegant design made from an elliptical enclosure, reversed script typography, a decorative pattern and a small decorative ornament. **[G]** A dimensional fabrication whose type has been cut from its uppermost layer. Illustrator's PATHFINDER operations were used to sculpt the upper and lower panels of this design, Gradient controls were used to color the panels' interiors and drop shadows were added to separate the design's layers while lifting them from the page.

A

B

C

D

E

F

G

Incorporating images with type

Visual conveyances ranging from plain to complex, from classic to cutting-edge and from silly to serious can be expressed through typographic and pictorial elements that have been incorporated into emblem-like designs. The challenge for designers (and a fun challenge it is) lies in choosing the right combination of pictorial and typographic material to portray the logo's targeted personality and to wrap everything with an enclosure that appropriately supports the design's visual and thematic expressions.

The first four samples on the opposite page—though clearly not alike—were all developed within exactly the same elliptical footprint. Why the presentation of four not-like finishes that all grew from an in-common beginning? It's to serve as a reminder that no matter where a project begins, it can end up absolutely anywhere you want to take it.

[A] This logo's icon gains visual emphasis through its dimensional appearance and also because of its border-breaking position along the edge of the design. **[B]** How about featuring your client's name as part of an illustration? The exaggerated halftone treatment of this design's pictorial content, the use of drastically dissimilar typefaces and the contrast apparent between the logo's crisp lettering and its soft-focus image amount to a contemporary and countercultural presentation. **[C]** The large symbol used in this dimensional enclosure has been layered between the design's dimensionally shaded backdrop and its solidly lettered type. **[D]** Bold sans serif capitals that loosely orbit a crudely rendered backdrop, a posterized illustration of a raised fist brandishing a sharpened pencil and a boldly stenciled acronym that hints at lofty goals: Conveyances of individuality, rebellion and purpose abound in this design. **[E]** Got an illustration that you could use as an enclosure for your client's name? If not, how about creating one?

A

B

C

D

E

251

Enclosing with decoration

Most designers would agree, there's something ultimately satisfying about encasing a beautifully rendered typeface with exquisitely crafted surroundings: It's like enclosing an ideally chosen gift with the perfect wrapping paper.

Where can designers go for the inspiration—and the raw materials—necessary to create enclosures that are attractive enough to be worthy of the typography they surround? Printed catalogs of copyright-free decorative and archival enclosure designs are an excellent place to start. Not only do these catalogs offer all kinds of inspirational ideas, they also offer ready-to-scan artwork that might fit the needs of a project you are working on.

Fonts of typographic ornaments can also be excellent sources of border-building elements (sample **[D]** was made by assembling a string of slightly modified typographic ornaments) as can Illustrator's well-stocked Symbols panel (sample **[C]** makes use of one of this panel's designs).

[A] By default, the blend mode of Photoshop's Outer Glow effect is set to "Screen" (a setting that is useful for adding a light glow against a dark background). Here, the effect's blend mode has been changed to "Multiply" so that it can be used to generate a softly colored blur around the forms of an ornate enclosure. **[B]** Small triangular extensions have been added to the tops and bottoms of this design's letters—decorations that add a subtle note of connection between the logo's typography and its ornate enclosure. **[C]** Old-style decorative designs have been merged with a rectangle to produce this classic-yet-contemporary enclosure. The bold gray outline around the design helps boost conveyances of modernity. **[D]** The tail of this logo's lowercase e has been extended into a type-enclosing train of leaves. A quiet sense of animation has been added to the design by allowing the last few leaves of the procession to depart from the others—as if carried off by wind. **[E]** A contemporary enclosure made from translucent layers of heavy swirls sitting over the top of a cloud-shaped solid. **[F]** The thorny look of this logo's decorative enclosure infuses the design with an edgy sense of modernity. The logo's subtext has been flowed along a curved path to draw attention to the implied dimensionality of the design.

A | B

C | D

E | F

253

Going big

Every once in a while designers find themselves enjoying a project that—instead of being limited by restrictions—seems only bound by rhetorical questions such as "Why not?" and "What's stopping me?" Are you working for a client who has granted you the green light for a no-holds-barred emblem design? If so, then how about throwing everything but the kitchen sink into your creation? (And what the heck, go ahead and use a kitchen sink if it improves the design. Why not? What's stopping you?)

Three rules of work: Out of clutter, find simplicity.

From discord, find harmony.

In the middle of difficulty lies opportunity.

Albert Einstein

Don't say you don't have enough time. You have exactly

the same number of hours per day that were given

to Helen Keller, Michelangelo, Leonardo da Vinci,

Mother Teresa, Thomas Jefferson and Albert Einstein.

H. Jackson Brown, Jr.

Design is a tough field, but it can also be rewarding and satisfying. If you want to stick around at least long enough to be handed juicy and fun creative tasks like designing logos for dynamic start-up companies, then you'll need to learn how to handle the job's challenges: tight deadlines, irritating coworkers, nagging clients and long hours, to name a few. The skills needed to rise above these challenges aren't necessarily covered in art school, so spend time and thought looking into—and implementing—on-the-job (and at-home) practices that will help you keep a sense of order and calm in the face of apparent calamity. Strange advice coming from a book about logos? Yes, but practical, too: These are the things that can keep you from burning out—and longevity and experience matter plenty when it comes to mastering any profession.

257

Constructing with type

How about assembling your client's name, tagline and even their address into a message-bearing typographic emblem—a design finalized with a deft application of color and the possible inclusion of linework and ornamentation? The emblem could be built using one font or several. The logo's characters could be presented as they are, modified to fit together in a creative way or treated to decorative extensions (like the drawn-out tail of the *R* in [A]). The design's type sizes could be kept consistent or they could be varied to generate visual interest and to establish a sense of hierarchy among the composition's elements. All or some of the typography's baselines could be curved, warped or tilted in order to lend shape and visual interest to the design. Take advantage of your computer's flexible typesetting and transformation tools and work through compositional possibilities such as these as you look for effective ways of presenting your typographic construction.

[A] An elegant and airy typographic emblem: The role of white space in conveying the refined visual personality of this design is no less crucial than that being played by its tasteful lettering. [B] A hard-to-ignore signature made through an in-your-face construction of mixed typefaces and a strong application of colors and shades. [C] The tagline of this vertical assemblage has been granted nearly as much visual emphasis as its company name—a historically inclined arrangement that echoes the look of the design's faux-aged letters. [D] Restrained stylishness and tasteful simplicity: A typographic construction made from generously kerned characters and thin horizontal rules. [E] It's not always easy to get words to overlap in an attractive and readable way, and usually, a fair amount of character customization needs to be performed in order to pull it off cleanly, but when it works, the outcome can be an agreeable and cohesive block of appealing typographic components. Is this an approach worth looking into for your current project? If so, then start stacking words and seeing how things go. [F] What about constructing the words of a slogan, catchphrase or headline into a logo-like typographic assemblage?

GREAT BLUE

H·E·R·O·N

Portland, Oregon

ART GALLERY

13th Annual

DUCK,

DODGE & DIVE

water balloon
fight AND

neighborhood
barbeque

theClever
STORK

ALEHOUSE
AND IMPORTER
OF EXTRAVAGANT
DELECTIBLES
FROM AROUND
THE GLOBE

A   B   C

CONTEMPORARY WATERFRONT CONDOMINIUMS

Sandpiper

17501 EAST RIVERBANK ROAD • BOSTON • MA

D

NOT ALL UGLY
ducklings
GROW UP AS

SWANS

BUT ALL HAVE
THE POTENTIAL
OF GROWING UP
beautiful

HANDCRAFTED BED COVERS SINCE 1933

SNOW
GOOSE

Down-filled quilts & comforters

VANCOUVER ISLAND, BRITISH COLUMBIA

E   F

Using type to enclose

Typography brackets or encloses the symbols appearing within this spread's signatures, and even though each of the logos uses in-common visual and typographic elements, the look of each design adheres to its own set of aesthetic and thematic goals. Use these samples to help brainstorm for ways of framing icons with type and also to reinforce the notion that there are endless ways of adapting compositional components to fit the specific needs of any design project.

CARTER DENTON

CUTLERY

BRUSSELS · MILAN · PARIS · LOS ANGELES

CARTER DENTON

Precision Swiss Timepieces

GUARANTEED AND STATE CERTIFIED

carter denton

INSTITUTIONAL FOOD SERVICES

CARTER

DENTON

WORLDWIDE ARCHIVAL SERVICES

est. 1937

CARTER DENTON

CARTER DENTON

BALTIMORE   MARYLAND

INVESTMENT ANALYSIS

carter

URBAN   STYLE

denton

261

Inside and out

Most of this chapter's samples feature components that sit either inside or outside the boundaries of enclosing elements. But how about thinking both inside *and* outside the box? What about coming up with a design whose elements sometimes obey and sometimes ignore the confines of their enclosures? And why not ignore a few more self-imposed restrictions while you're at it? How about using a mixture of illustrative techniques, combining unalike typefaces and employing visual styles that come from more than one era?

[A] With enough decoration, color and typographic variety, even a highly structured symmetrical arrangement of elements can convey Bohemian qualities of nonconformity and quirkiness. **[B]** A typography-wrapped backdrop sitting behind an illustrated bicycle that ignores the boundaries of its enclosure: In this design, visual impact and aesthetic drama take priority over obedience to strict structural rules. **[C]** Three completely unalike fonts and two dissimilar styles of illustration went into the construction of this emblem—a design that simultaneously projects conveyances of modernity while paying homage to the past. **[D]** Over, under, around and inside: This signature's main typography brackets the design's innermost symbol while resting within enclosing background shapes.

Color is a very important consideration when it comes to putting the finishing touches on an emblem design. Chapter 7, Color, beginning on page 268, provides palette-building ideas that can be applied to emblems as well as to any other kind of logo design.

NORTHEASTERN COASTAL TOUR
JULY 21 THROUGH AUGUST 7

CELESTIAL CYCLES INC.
AUSTIN TX.

A | B
C | D

PLANETARY
coffee COMPANY
"Unearthly goodness since 1988"

UNIVERSAL
KALEIDOSCOPE COMPANY

263

Exercises

Use the samples throughout The Logo Brainstorm Book *to help generate ideas as you seek solutions for these exercises. Make an effort to push your ideas into fresh creative territory—from thumbnail to finish.*

If you are interested in adding color to any of the designs you create for these exercises, consider checking out chapter 7, Color, pages 268–296, for tips and ideas.

CREATING ENCLOSURES

See all the empty enclosure designs on pages 246–247? Now it's your turn. If you are already competent using Illustrator's shape-construction tools then this exercise will give you a chance to show your stuff while sharpening your skills. If you are new to Illustrator, or inexperienced with its drawing tools, then this is the perfect exercise for you: Not only will you gain experience with a critically important set of tools, you will also end up with a potentially useful set of enclosures that could be adapted to fit the needs of future logo projects.

- Produce between twelve and fifteen ready-for-use enclosures.

- Some of your designs should have large open areas and others should be divided into subpanels where words or images could be placed.

- Produce enclosures that are contemporary, casual, free-form and geometric.

- Come up with at least one design that is rendered in an ornate and classic style.

- Include linework in some of your creations.

- Vary the proportions of your enclosures. Some should lean toward horizontal, others vertical and others square or round.

- Include at least a couple of ribbons or banners in your designs. (Banners and ribbons are the focus of this section's third exercise, and examples of these design components are shown in yellow on pages 246–247.)

- Aim for a good degree of variety among your custom-crafted enclosures.

- Colors may be applied to your designs.

- Save all of your creations for possible future use.

DIMENSIONAL TREATMENTS

As an optional extension of the previous exercise, convert three of your custom-built enclosures into strongly dimensional designs. Consider using drop shadows, dimensional effects (such as Illustrator's Warp effects or Photoshop's Bevel and Emboss treatments), 3-D rendering software or illustration techniques that project illusions of depth. Save these designs along with those from the first exercise.

TWISTS AND TURNS

Banners and ribbons can be added to emblems—as well as to nonemblem logos—as a way of adding a touch of decorative flair, to introduce feelings of dimension and to add connotations of nostalgia.

Why not spend some time sharpening your banner and ribbon creation skills? Not only can these skills be applied when rendering the twists and turns of subjects made from things like cloth, rubber, leather or pasta, they can also be called upon to create reality-altering depictions of things that are normally rigid, such as buildings that fold like shirts or pencils that bend into pretzels.

- Begin this exercise with research. Do a web search for "banner illustrations" (also, see pages 246–247 for basic examples of ribbons and banners) and you'll probably be surprised by the variety of ways in which these subjects can be illustrated, the range of styles in which they can be depicted and the fact that they seem to have been in continuous use as visual garnish from the Byzantine era onward. Use the images you find to educate yourself about the ways that shapes and shading can be used to depict the form, flow and dimension of these graphic elements.

- Next, use pens, pencils, paint or the computer (or a mix of tools) to create a dozen banners and/or ribbons. Your renderings need not be finalized—just develop your ideas a step or two beyond the thumbnail stage so that they could be used as ready-to-go reference if you decide to finish and use some of your designs for a project one day.

- Create at least a few banners that could be used to hold type or images—though there is no need to add either of these things to your designs for now.

- Save your sketches and digital creations for possible reference and finalization in the future.

EMBLEM CREATION

You'll need a symbol or a representational icon from one of the exercises at the end of chapter 2 for this exercise. If you haven't already done one of those exercises, then select a nice looking typographic ornament from an existing typeface and use that as an icon.

This project involves the creation of three different enclosures that each include a pictorial element plus a fictitious company name.

- Come up with a multiword company name to go with your symbol, icon or typographic ornament and develop two enclosed emblem designs using these elements.

- Enclosures from one of the previous exercises may be used for this project.

- The exterior shape of each of the emblems should be relatively square or circular. (The designs' elements may protrude slightly beyond their enclosures.)

- One design should incorporate black or colored linework. The other should have no linework.

- One of the emblems should be designed to grant compositional prominence to its symbol, icon or typographic ornament. The other should feature its typographic elements most strongly.

- Consider adding subtle background patterns and decorative elements to your designs. Special effects of any kind can also be used.

PURELY TYPOGRAPHIC

A theatre company that produces works aimed at school-age audiences is about to launch a season of plays based on Aesop's fables. An educational booklet is being produced for audience members and the client would like to feature quotations from the fables inside the booklet.

- The client has asked for two typographic constructions (more or less along the lines of the final sample on page 259) made using quotes from Aesop's fables.

- Pick up a book of Aesop's fables or do a web search for "Aesop quotes." Look through your findings for two quotations that you think will adapt themselves well to typographic constructions.

- The designs should fit within 4" x 5.5" vertical spaces.

- The two constructions should look distinctly different from each other, and, at the same time, they should go together well as a pair. (Trust your artistic instinct to tell you how to pull this off.)

- More than one font may be used for each design. You may also use the same font(s) for both constructions—as long as the individuality of each design is maintained.

- Small typographic ornaments may be incorporated but no other forms of decoration, imagery or linework are to be included.

- Keep your school-age audience in mind: The look of your designs could be literary but should not come across as stuffy; the style could be formal but not without hints of playfulness.

- Color may be applied to the designs.

AN EMBLEM TO CALL YOUR OWN

There are few guidelines for this exercise. The job is simply this:

- Produce an emblem-style design based on an interest that you are passionate about. For example, if you are a fan of vintage cars, then a design could be built around something like the image of a 1967 Chevy Corvette; if music is your thing then you might choose to include the silhouette of a Stradivarius violin or a Stratocaster guitar in your emblem; if you are an avid ornithologist (a.k.a. a lover of birds) then perhaps you'd choose to decoratively depict a pileated woodpecker as the centerpiece of your creation.

- Use whatever software or hands-on tools you prefer to build your design.

- Anything goes. Your emblem may contain words, photos, illustrations, icons, patterns, decorations, linework and ornaments. Special effects may be applied to any or all of your design's elements.

- Color your emblem with a palette of hues that is especially attractive to you.

7   Color

CHAPTER CONTENTS

7   Color

ARE THERE EFFECTIVE WAYS of combining colors using something other than vague feelings that seem to suggest that certain hues go well together and that others don't? There certainly are, and these color-picking strategies are based on age-old methods that are as effective at coming up with eye-catching and trend-setting palettes today as they were during the Renaissance.

The palette-building methods presented in this chapter are based on three easy-to-grasp components. The first is a tried-and-true set of associations between hues on the color wheel: monochromatic, complementary, split complementary, analo-

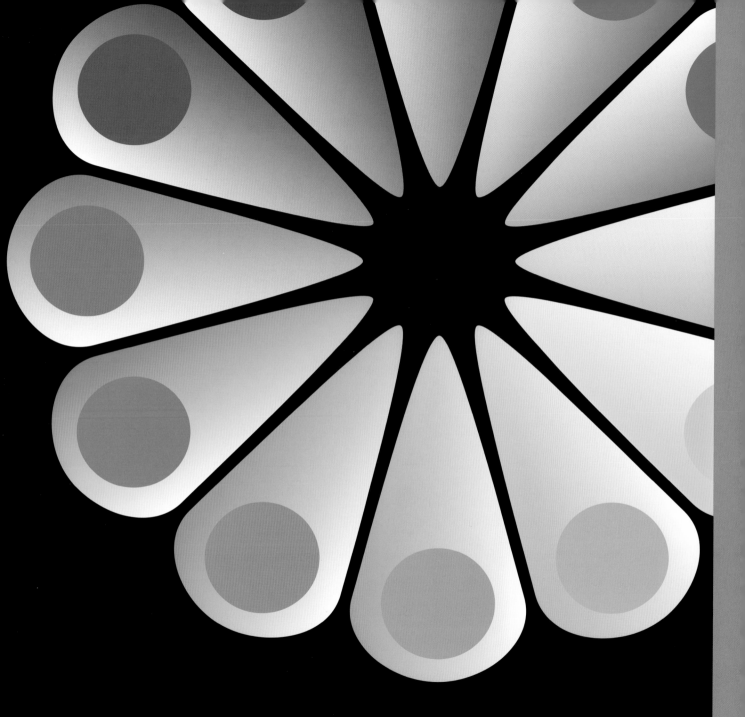

gous and triadic (each of these kinds of color relation-ships are defined on the pages ahead). The second is the all-important knowledge that any hue can be featured as a value that ranges from dark to light and with saturation that ranges from bright to muted. The third component for the effective application of color is an awareness of current color trends—a consciousness that's been cultivated by keeping your eyes open to the palettes used by today's outstanding artists and designers.

How would you rate your color-picking confidence? Do you feel fully competent, moderately capable or completely in the dark? However you answer this question, there is something in this chapter for you—whether its content serves as a refresher on the concepts that underlie your well-honed palette-building skills, whether it helps solidify the thinking behind your developing color-combining instincts or whether it provides you with just the set of fundamentals you've been looking for upon which to build your own color-savvy sensibilities.

The vocabulary of color:

Hue: another word for color

Saturation: the brightness or purity of a color (also referred to as *intensity*)

Value: the relative lightness or darkness of a hue on a scale from white to black

One color plus black

Printing budgets, client preferences and project goals often dictate that a logo be limited to a single spot color (a specific color of ink that's premixed before it's loaded into a printing press) plus black ink. Still, this limit doesn't need to be seen as a restriction: An effectively chosen color—combined with black and applied appropriately to a well-crafted logo—should be more than capable of helping the signature attract and hold the attention of its target audience.

[A] Working with just one color plus black? Brainstorm your options: It may surprise you to find out just how many ways a logo can be colored and shaded using a limited palette. **[B]** Consider solutions that range from muted to bright. **[C]** Three options to consider whenever you're deciding how to apply a spot color (plus the option of black ink) to a logo-plus-icon design: apply color to the icon and use black for the type, present the type in color and make the icon black or use the spot color for everything. **[D]** Got a favored hue in mind? Use the computer to see how your logo looks when it is colored with an intense form of the hue and also take a look at how the design comes across when it's treated to lighter, darker and less saturated versions of the color. (Adobe's Color Picker panel—featured at the bottom of page 288—is a useful tool for exploring variations of any hue).

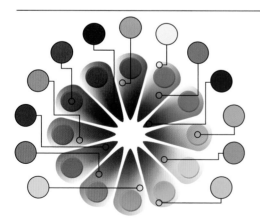

Faced with an infinite number of choices, how do you know which color is right for the logo you're working on? By paying attention: Take note of color trends of the present, the past and the (projected) future, become familiar with the media your target audience enjoys, investigate the way your client's competition uses color (not for the sake of copying, but for the sake of choosing something different) and be mindful as to which colors are—and which colors are not—well suited to the media in which the logo will be presented.

A

B

C

D

Monochromatic

Monochromatic sets of colors tend to convey themselves more quietly than other palettes (complementary, triadic, analogous, etc.). This is because the amount of variety within monochromatic schemes is limited to differences in value and intensity, while other kinds of palettes can also take advantage of differences between hues.

Would a visually subdued palette fit the thematic and visual goals of the logo you're working on? If so, then consider coloring the design with a set of monochromatic hues—with or without the addition of black and/or white elements.

[A] A trio of logos colored with monochromatic hues along with black and white (black and white are usually considered permissible additions to monochromatic palettes). If you are choosing colors for an icon that will be used as a backdrop for typography, consider applying a monochromatic palette to the backdrop design. Monochromatic color combinations—because of their low-key visual impact—are well suited for graphic elements that are meant to present themselves in a non-distracting way. **[B]** How about delineating your design's monochromatic hues with black or white lines? Differences in value can also be relied upon to clearly distinguish a palette's shades. **[C]** Screened tints of any color of ink count as that color's monochromatic relatives. Consider expanding your spot-color (or your spot-color-plus-black) palette by including tints of the ink(s).

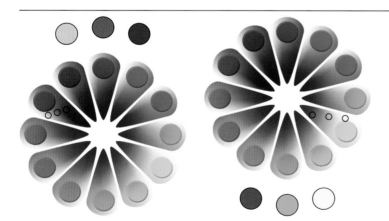

Monochromatic palettes are sets of hues taken from a single spoke of the color wheel. The colors in a monochromatic palette can differ by value, by intensity or by both value and intensity.

Complementary

Complementary colors come from opposite sides of the color wheel and have absolutely nothing in common: There is no red in green, no yellow in violet, and blue contains nary a trace of orange. Why are pairs of colors with nothing in common described as "complementary"? Perhaps it's because both hues in a complementary pair can express themselves in precisely all the ways that the other cannot, and pairs of complementary hues can therefore convey themselves with a spectral wholeness that's beyond the reach of any other type of color pairing.

Looking for an ultimately dynamic duo of hues for your logo? Look no further than a pair of complementary hues.

[A] Investigating ways of applying a pair of complementary hues to a logo? Consider solutions that feature different amounts of each color as well as ideas that include screens of one or both inks. [B] Intense? Muted? Lightened? Darkened? Use the computer to explore differences in saturation and value before deciding which incarnation of each of your complementary hues looks best. [C] How about muting one of the hues of your complementary palette and featuring the other at full intensity? Magenta and yellow-green take turns playing muted and bright roles in this pair of designs. [D] Magenta and yellow-green appear in these logos as well. Both hues appear at full intensity in the first sample, and in the second design the yellow-green has been lightened as a way of granting clear visual emphasis to the signature's bright and saturated central icon.

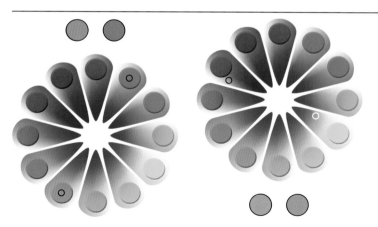

Complementary hues come from opposite segments of the color wheel. When pairing complementary colors, try using both hues at full strength, and also see how the combination is affected when one or both of the colors are muted, lightened or darkened.

Tip: There's no need to be exact when choosing a pair of complementary hues (or when selecting colors for any of the other palettes featured in this chapter). Let your design sense guide you toward hues that fit the general description of the kind of palette being formed and don't hesitate to make adjustments to any of the palette's colors if you feel that the adjustments improve the look and the effect of their combined presence.

A

B

C

D

279

Split complementary

Want to come up with an eye-catching multicolor palette for your logo? A combination of hues that delivers connotations of both harmony and contrast? Consider a split-complementary palette—a palette built from two harmoniously related near neighbors and one contrasting hue from the other side of the color wheel.

When building a split-complimentary palette (or any other kind of palette, for that matter), explore variations that involve muting some of its colors, breaking its hues down into multiple shades and varying its colors' values to achieve different degrees of contrast.

[A] Once you have a logo at least roughly designed, and a set of split-complementary hues chosen and ready for application, your next task should be to try out all kinds of different color configurations. Software makes creative exploration of this kind too easy to pass up. **[B]** Two designs—one with a graphic colored using close-value split-complementary hues and one that features colors of widely different values. Close-value palettes tend to deliver themselves with more restraint than their wide-valued relatives. **[C]** The hues of a split-complementary palette have been variously shuffled to produce the coloring for this signature's trio of icons. **[D]** Unless printing restrictions forbid it, why not consider adding gray, black or white to your split-complementary color scheme?

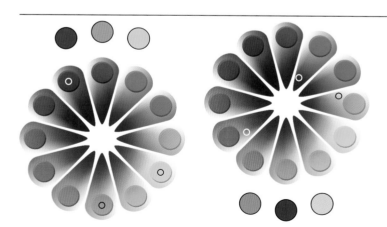

Split-complementary palettes are built by choosing a color and pairing it with the two hues on either side of the original color's complement. The hues within a split-complementary palette can be used full intensity, muted, lightened or darkened.

A

B

C

D

281

When I'm working on a problem,
I never think about beauty. I think
only how to solve the problem. But
when I have finished, if the solution
is not beautiful, I know it is wrong.

Richard Buckminster Fuller

Color is only beautiful

when it means something.

Robert Henri

The logo you've just created has everything it needs to be considered beautiful: Its typeface is a perfectly chosen and ideally displayed font, its icon is an exquisitely rendered symbol that conveys its powerful meaning through elegant aesthetics and the design as a whole has been crafted for maximum appeal before the eyes of its audience. What could possibly ruin the logo at this point? Poorly chosen colors, that's what. After all, if a logo's colors are repulsive, then it's extremely doubtful that either the signature's content or its aesthetics will ever have a chance to wow their viewers. How does a designer avoid ruining a good thing when applying colors to a logo? By looking into the tastes of the design's audience and finding out what colors these people find attractive, meaningful, timely and relevant. In other words, by finding out what colors the target audience finds beautiful.

Analogous

Anthropomorphically speaking, analogous palettes are akin to groups of like-minded individuals who are united toward a common cause: similar but different, individualistic but united. The individual colors of an analogous palette—because they are linked by their status as neighbors on the color wheel—are able to work together to convincingly amplify certain thematic expressions—as when bright shades of yellow, yellow-orange and orange are used to transmit feelings of energy and life, or when toned-down incarnations of blue-green, blue and blue-violet are combined to deliver conveyances of a quiet and soothing nature.

[A] Cool vs. warm: The first of these designs has been colored with an analogous set of hues from a cool portion of the spectrum while the other has been painted with hues from the warmer side of the color wheel (the neutral browns and tans in this sample were created by muting orange, orange-red and orange-yellow hues). **[B]** How about using a bright set of analogous hues to enliven an otherwise all-black signature? What about leaving black out of the picture and coloring the design with only analogous hues? Would a simple enclosure or the inclusion of white help produce the kind of outcome you're looking for? **[C]** When adding black to any set of colors, try out different roles for the black ink. Should it outline all or some of the design's major components? Should it strongly outline just a central element or illustration? Would the palette gel better if its black was screened to one or more shades of gray?

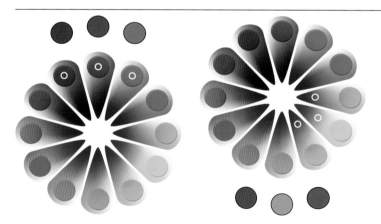

Analogous hues are neighbors on the color wheel. Analogous palettes may be built from colors that are similarly saturated and they can also include hues that are various degrees of intensity and value.

A

B

C

285

Triadic

Triadic palettes are combinations of hues that come from equally spaced spokes of the color wheel. Highly saturated triadic combinations (intense violets, greens and oranges, for example) tend to convey themselves in a lively manner since each of the palette's colors is notably different from the others. High-energy triadic schemes are often used for marketing material aimed at younger audiences and at adults who are interested in sports, travel and adventure.

Triadic combinations of a more sophisticated nature can made by muting one or more of the palette's hues and by including notably pale and/or dark shades.

[A] The red used in this triadic palette is featured at nearly full intensity, the blue has been slightly muted and the yellow has been dulled considerably in the logo's lower region: Explore variations in saturation and value when combining triadic hues. (Black has been allowed into this triadic palette—just as it has been allowed into each of the chapter's other palettes.) [B] A dark and dusty shade of blue has taken the place of black in this presentation of muted triadic relatives. [C] This sample's colors have been muted considerably—almost to the point of becoming neutrals and grays. [D] Isn't the sky supposed to be blue? Yes ... but not always. The computer makes it easy to swap the arrangement of colors in a design or an illustration in search of intriguing alternatives to normalcy.

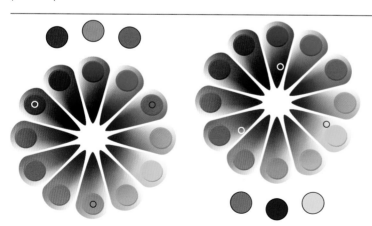

Triadic palettes are made from hues taken from equally spaced spokes of the color wheel. Experiment with various amounts of saturation and different values when working with triadic combinations.

A | B
C | D

287

Semi-muted

Where bright colors shout, muted tones might converse quietly or even whisper. Where highly saturated colors speak with authority and directness, muted shades might convey themselves with humility, restraint or mystery. Intense palettes almost always say, "See me: Here I am,"— whether their colors are seen on a brand new car or on an abandoned wreck. A muted palette, on the other hand, might say one thing if it's used to color a new car's elegant interior, and quite another thing if it's used to portray the torn and damaged insides of a junkyard heap.

What exactly do you want your logo to say? Would the straightforward and energetic qualities of a bright palette speak its message best? What about using the sometimes sophisticated, sometimes mysterious and sometimes begrimed voice of a muted collection of hues instead? How about employing a bit of both and allowing, for example, a set of darkly muted hues to quietly set the stage for the radiant persona of a fully saturated accent color? Take cues from the work of great designers and trust your artistic instinct as you explore your options.

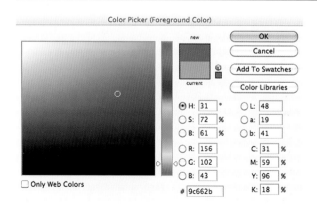

When painters want to mute a color, they generally mix the hue with its complement, with black or with a shade of gray. How do designers use the computer to investigate muted, lightened or darkened versions of a hue? One excellent tool for finding these variations is the Color Picker panel offered through Photoshop and Illustrator. Use your mouse to click on points within the panel's large colored square to explore variations of any hue's value and/or saturation.

Heavily muted

Each of the palettes described in this chapter could be used as the basis for a heavily muted set of hues. When applying any palette of strongly muted colors to a logo, keep in mind that palettes of this kind are context sensitive. A darkened set of dusty grays and browns, for instance, if applied to a weathered-looking urban-style logo, might deliver contemporary connotations of wear and tear. However, if the same set of muted tones were applied to the gracefully rendered emblem of an upscale wine bar, conveyances of wealth and repose might ensue.

[A] How muted is muted enough? Explore your options by taking advantage of the Color Picker feature in Illustrator or Photoshop to identify and try different levels of saturation for your design's toned-down hues. **[B]** Tinted grays have been used to color these scalloped enclosures. Two of the designs feature grays that lean toward the warm end of the spectrum and one has been colored using a cool gray. The samples' other colors—though also restrained in saturation—appear relatively bright because of their proximity to the heavily muted grays. **[C]** A trio of subdued palettes worth considering if you are limited to one color plus black: black plus a low-intensity hue, a screen of black ink plus a saturated hue and black plus a screen of itself paired with a strongly muted color.

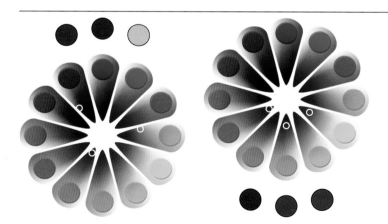

Browns, warm grays (grays that tend toward brown, red, yellow or orange) and cool grays (grays that lean toward green, blue or violet) are actually highly muted versions of ordinary hues.

MADHOUSE COFFEE + CULTURE

MADHOUSE COFFEE + CULTURE

MADHOUSE COFFEE + CULTURE

A

B

C

Exercises

Use the samples throughout The Logo Brainstorm Book *to help generate ideas as you seek solutions for these exercises. Make an effort to push your ideas into fresh creative territory—from thumbnail to finish.*

Note: You will need to use logos from one of this book's earlier exercises for some of this section's projects.

REAL-WORLD COLOR

Extra attention is devoted to this chapter's opening exercise. Why the added emphasis? It's because this project involves media that many designers are not at all familiar with, and also because it's *that* important.

Designers who have worked with actual paints and brushes tend to be among the most fearless of their kind when it comes to choosing, combining and altering colors with both real-world and digital tools. This is probably because the brain often learns best when it learns through multisensory experiences, and there's no better

way to learn inarguable lessons about color than by picking up a brush and painting with actual pigments on real-life surfaces of paper, canvas and cardboard.

- Mixing pigments teaches designers exactly what needs to be done to lighten, darken, mute or intensify hues. Working with paint also teaches designers how to convert one color into another.

- Blending pigments makes it clear how in-common color components can be used to create harmonious palettes (by adding a small amount of blue-gray, for example, to a green, a yellow and a gray to help the three colors visually connect).

- The experience of mixing colors using tubes of paint heightens a designer's awareness of how the colors in everyday life come about and how those colors can be replicated using both pigments and pixels.

Interested in boosting your aptitude with—and your awareness of—color? Then paint. Few supplies are needed to get started and the following list of supplies has been targeted specifically at designers who want to deepen their understanding of the ways of color:

- One tube each of Titanium White, Primary Cyan, Primary Magenta, Primary Yellow and Ivory Black acrylic paints from Golden Acrylics. Why these paints? It's because Golden Acrylics has formulated these water-soluble cyan, magenta, yellow and black paints to behave like CMYK printing inks—a formulation that makes them extremely relevant to graphic designers.

- A container of matte or gloss acrylic medium. These mediums are used to thin acrylic paints and to varnish finished paintings.

- Optionally, a container of gesso (a white paint that dries with a slightly toothy texture). Gesso can be used to prepare surfaces prior to painting them with acrylics.

- One or two inexpensive nylon brushes.

- A pad of thick watercolor paper or a sheet of cold-press illustration board cut into small rectangles (approx. 8" x 10").

- Something to mix paints on: a palette, an old dinner plate or a small piece of Plexiglas.

- A jar of water and a roll of paper towels.

And now for a couple of straightforward exercises, projects that should prove enlightening—especially to those who have never painted before.

- First of all, copy the above color wheel with your paints. (Don't worry about precisely duplicating the wheel's form or about making its outline sharp and precise: concentrate instead on accurately depicting the colors of the wheel's segments.) Start by painting the blue, red and yellow spokes of the color wheel, then mix these colors to produce the green, violet and orange slices. After that, further mix your colors to produce the remaining segments. Aim for smooth visual jumps as your hues step from one slice to another and take the time to fine-tune your work until it is as accurate as you can make it.

- Create a second version of the color wheel, only this time, mix hues that are muted similarly to those shown above.

- A color can be muted by mixing it with its complement (the color directly opposite a hue on the color wheel) or by mixing it with a neutral gray or brown.

- Don't worry about matching the above-shown colors precisely for this project: simply aim for an attractive wheel of consistently muted colors.

Beyond these exercises, the next steps are up to you. What about keeping your art supplies handy and creating simple abstractions and basic still-life paintings for fun during your nonworking hours? You will be amazed at what you can learn about color when creating images with paints—and you'll probably be very pleased when, after a few weeks or months, you suddenly discover that you've got a stack of ready-to-frame pieces of art for your home or office.

BLACK PLUS ONE

A logo that you created for an earlier chapter's exercise will be needed for this project.

Designers are often asked to finalize a logo using the cost-effective palette of black ink plus one spot color (often a color from the Pantone Matching System). This exercise invites you to experience and meet the oft-faced challenge of selecting and applying black and one color of ink to a logo design. Are you feeling unsure about the potential for creativity when limited to one color of ink plus black? Take a look at the nine samples at the top of page 275: As you can see, "limiting" yourself to a palette such as this is hardly limiting at all.

- Import your logo into Illustrator and choose a Pantone color for your design. (If possible, choose your color from one of Pantone's printed guides since the accuracy of on-screen colors can't be guaranteed.)

- Having trouble selecting a color? Not having trouble? Either way, it would be an excellent idea to look through design annuals and contemporary media to refresh your awareness of what colors are at the fore of today's media.

Choose a color that boosts the communicative powers of your design in a way that's in step with current tastes.

- Try out different ways of applying your chosen color and black to your logo and consider applying either ink as one or more screened percentage.

- When you come up with a solution you like, put a copy of the design aside and continue looking for additional ways of coloring your creation.

- Add an enclosure or a background panel to your design if you want to expand the ways in which color can be applied.

- Repeat this procedure until you have produced no less than nine distinct variations of the design. Be determined and resourceful as you work: Don't give in even if it starts to feel like you've exhausted all possibilities (rest assured—you haven't).

PALETTE STRATEGIES

An emblem from one of the exercises at the end of chapter 6 would be ideal for this project—either that or an enclosed signature from another chapter's exercise.

Here's your chance to put into practice several of this chapter's palette-building strategies. Here, monochromatic, complementary, split-complementary, analogous and triadic schemes will be applied to an emblem (or any other kind of enclosed logo) that you created for a previous section's exercise.

- Select one of your emblem or enclosed-signature creations and open it in Illustrator.

- Create five versions of your design—one for each of these kinds of palettes: monochromatic, complementary, split-complementary, analogous and triadic.

- CMYK colors should be used for this exercise. If possible, choose your colors from a printed resource that includes samples along with CMYK formulas. Remember: It's rarely a good idea to choose colors based on how they appear on your monitor.

- Regardless of which kind of palette you are applying, it's usually best to begin by selecting a "starter hue." This hue will be the foundational member of your cast of colors, and, depending on its position on the color wheel, it will determine the general area from which the palette's supporting hues will come.

- Trust your best aesthetic judgment when selecting colors for your palettes: Absolute scientific accuracy is not mandatory when choosing these hues.

- Pay particular attention to the value and the level of saturation of each color in your palettes. Aim for pleasing associations between your selected hues that allow them to effectively express—as a group— the logo's sought-after conveyances.

- Aim for a good measure of variety among the color schemes you apply: Work as though your goal was to show the client an exceptionally wide range of plausible colorings for their logo.

MUTING

Imagine that the outcomes from the previous exercise were presented and that the client was pleased. Well, almost: The logo committee loved the brightest and most

colorful of the designs, but the company's CEO (a man known for his contrary nature) wants to take a look at the selected design with some or all of its colors muted—just for the sake of comparison.

- Select your brightest and most colorful design from the preceding exercise and open it in Illustrator.

- Mute all but one of the design's hues and then raise the saturation of the unmuted color to its brightest level. Finalize the design by adjusting the distribution of its hues in a way that limits the role of the bright color to that of an intense but minimally appearing accent color.

- Develop another variation of the design where all of its hues are strongly muted—but not to the point where the colors lose their original essence. If necessary, adjust the colors' values to keep the overall palette from becoming too dark.

- And lastly, create a version of the emblem that features hues that are each so heavily muted that they become various shades of grays and browns.

Check out these other great books from Jim Krause

DESIGN ESSENTIALS INDEX

Combining three invaluable reference books for idea-hungry designers, *Design Essentials Index* offers everything from new color-combination systems to an in-depth examination of practical applications of type. This box set includes Jim Krause's best-selling *Design Basics Index*, *Type Idea Index* and *Color Index 2* to give designers a wealth of actionable information.

PHOTO IDEA INDEX: PEOPLE, PLACES AND THINGS

In the *Photo Idea Index* series, Jim Krause provides in-depth tips and tricks for using standard digital equipment to create professional-quality images. From photographing people from different perspectives to finding inspiration in sweeping views of natural and man-made environments to exploring objects in the world around you, *Photo Idea Index: People, Places* and *Things* will teach you how to capture awe-inspiring digital images.

Find these books and many others at MyDesignShop.com or your local bookstore.